Richmond Celia

Egypt, Greece, and Rome

Richmond Celia

Egypt, Greece, and Rome

ISBN/EAN: 9783337329921

Printed in Europe, USA, Canada, Australia, Japan

Cover: Foto ©ninafisch / pixelio.de

More available books at **www.hansebooks.com**

WORLD LITERATURE READERS

EGYPT, GREECE, AND ROME

BY

CELIA RICHMOND

GINN AND COMPANY
BOSTON · NEW YORK · CHICAGO · LONDON

PREFACE

The series of World Literature Readers, designed for use in Grades V-IX, aims to give a glimpse into the real life of the various nations of the world — to open a gate upon a path which, if the youthful explorer wills to follow it, may lead him on into wide fields.

He who has learned to read is no longer a citizen of one age or one land, but of all ages and all lands. Through literature and through art he may lose the boundaries of his own meager experience and win his way into the thoughts, ideals, aspirations, knowledge, and visions of the best minds of all times and races — the possessions of the entire human family. To realize our world heritage we need to touch the beginnings of things, in the folk tale and myth not only of our own people and land but of all peoples and lands; we need companionship with the heroes of the human race, — not only the heroes of war and adventure but the heroes of our common life, — for the race, as Hamilton Mabie says, "lives in its heroic folk, its men and women who dare and do, the ever-returning figure in its myths, traditions, epics, histories, novels."

Out of the common life, — out of the simple sensations that spring from sight of star-decked sky, of splendor of dawn and sunset, of storm and rain, of free, wild life of bird and beast; that spring from knowledge of the struggles of men and women who do the world's work, — out of this

WORLD LITERATURE READERS

common life have come the elements that flowered into beauty at the touch of the masters of music, literature, poetry, sculpture, architecture, and painting.

The youth of to-day cannot see our American land as it was in the days of our pioneer forefathers, nor England as it was in the time of Shakespeare, nor Egypt, Greece, and Rome as they thrilled to the touch of the ancient master builders, but through books and through art he may lay hold of the elements of those far-away lives and build them into a structure in the realm of the spirit, perhaps not unlike what Robinson and Brewster saw, what the seer of Stratford beheld, and Phidias and Rameses dreamed.

So the World Literature Readers attempt to bring into prominence the special characteristics and genius of each nation, the material used being drawn from stores of literature, history, and art — whatever can aid in presenting the particular gifts of each to the world.

The present volume attempts to make the life on which our English civilization is based as real and vital as possible. The Egyptian section touches upon the life and art of ancient Egypt, the mysteries of the desert, the Sphinx, and the pyramids; it gives stories from the life of Joseph and from the lives of the Israelites at the time of their bondage in Egypt, from the Arabian Nights, and from Plutarch. The Greek section includes vivid pictures of the Homeric idyls (the stories of Nausicaa and Ulysses and Jason, of Baucis and Philemon and Pandora, retold by Lamb and Kingsley and Hawthorne), hints as to the greatness of Greek art, and a touch of modern Greece. The Roman section gives a bit of the story of Æneas, and other tales from Roman mythology, descriptions of the Roman achievements in engineering, stories from the

PREFACE

life of Julius Cæsar, and extended selections from "The Last Days of Pompeii" and from Marcus Aurelius.

Grateful acknowledgment is made to the publishing houses whose kindness permitted the use of the following copyrighted material: selections from the writings of Ralph Waldo Emerson, Henry Wadsworth Longfellow, and Edna Dean Proctor, used by permission of, and by special arrangement with, Houghton Mifflin Company, authorized publishers of the works of these authors; "Springtime in Greece" and "A Modern Nausicaa," from "In Argolis," by George Horton (A. C. McClurg & Co.); "A Victor of the Games," from "A Victor of Salamis," by William Stearns Davis, and "The Temple of Castor and Pollux" and "The Roman Forum," from "Stories in Stone from the Roman Forum," by Isabel Lovell (The Macmillan Company); "The Child and the Wind," by Lucy Lyttleton (Thomas B. Mosher, publisher); "The Flight of Æneas," translated by Harlan H. Ballard (through the kindness of Mr. Ballard) (Charles Scribner's Sons); and "The Approach to the Desert," by Robert Smythe Hichens (Frederick A. Stokes Company).

CELIA RICHMOND

CONTENTS

EGYPT

	PAGE
THE RIVER NILE (from "Egypt, the Land of the Temple Builders") *Walter Scott Perry*	1
THE PYRAMIDS AND THE SPHINX (from "Nile Notes of a Howadji") *George William Curtis*	5
THE SPHINX SPEAKS . . . . *Francis Saltus Saltus*	12
THE APPROACH TO THE DESERT . . . *Robert Smythe Hichens*	15
THE TEMPLE OF KARNAK (from "Egypt, the Land of the Temple Builders") . . . . *Walter Scott Perry*	18
ABOU BEN ADHEM . . . . *Leigh Hunt*	24
THE STORY OF JOSEPH (from Genesis xxxvii–xlv)	25
THE SEVENTH PLAGUE OF EGYPT . . . . . *George Croly*	35
THE FISHERMAN AND THE GENIE (from The Arabian Nights) .	39
MERCY (from "The Merchant of Venice") *William Shakespeare*	53
THE SUN IN EGYPT (from "Nile Notes of a Howadji") *George William Curtis*	54
AN ORIENTAL BAZAAR (from "The Howadji in Syria") *George William Curtis*	57
THE COMING OF THE PERSIAN EMBASSY (from "An Egyptian Princess") . . . . *Georg Moritz Ebers*	62
THE STATUES OF MEMNON (from "Egypt, the Land of the Temple Builders") . . . . *Walter Scott Perry*	68
THE HOUSE OF RHODOPIS (from "An Egyptian Princess") *Georg Moritz Ebers*	70
ANTONY AND CLEOPATRA (from Plutarch's "Parallel Lives") . .	78
CLEOPATRA (from "Antony and Cleopatra") *William Shakespeare*	82
THE KNOWLEDGE OF THE ANCIENT EGYPTIANS	84
THE NUMBER OF THE STARS (from "Star-Land") *Sir Robert Stawell Ball*	87

WORLD LITERATURE READERS

	PAGE
THE WONDERS OF THE HEAVENS (from Psalm cxlvii and Job xxxviii)	89
THE CHILD AND THE WIND . . . . . . *Lucy Lyttleton*	90

GREECE

NAUSICAA (from the Odyssey of Homer) Translated by *William Cullen Bryant*	93
THE RETURN OF ULYSSES (from "The Adventures of Ulysses") *Charles Lamb*	107
HOW JASON WENT TO SCHOOL (from "The Argonauts") *Charles Kingsley*	114
THE SPARTANS' MARCH . . . . *Felicia Dorothea Hemans*	122
A VICTOR OF THE GAMES (from "A Victor of Salamis") *William Stearns Davis*	125
THE MIRACULOUS PITCHER (from "A Wonder-Book for Girls and Boys") . . . . *Nathaniel Hawthorne*	134
THE PARADISE OF CHILDREN (from "A Wonder-Book for Girls and Boys") . . . . *Nathaniel Hawthorne*	144
PERICLES (from Plutarch's "Parallel Lives")	153
THE PARTHENON	157
EARTH PROUDLY WEARS THE PARTHENON (from "The Problem") *Ralph Waldo Emerson*	158
THE RUINED PARTHENON (from "Travels in Greece") *Bayard Taylor*	160
IN ARCADY . . . . *Robert Louis Stevenson*	164
SPRINGTIME IN GREECE (from "In Argolis") . *George Horton*	166
A MODERN NAUSICAA (from "In Argolis") . *George Horton*	173
THE BOOK . . . . *Emily Dickinson*	177

ROME

THE FLIGHT OF ÆNEAS (from Vergil's Æneid) Translated by *Harlan H. Ballard*	179
THE SIBYLLINE BOOKS	185
THE TEMPLE OF CASTOR AND POLLUX (from "Stories in Stone from the Roman Forum") . . . . . . *Isabel Lovell*	189

CONTENTS

	PAGE
THE BATTLE OF LAKE REGILLUS (from "Lays of Ancient Rome") *Thomas Babington Macaulay*	193
CROSSING THE RUBICON (from "A Friend to Cæsar") *William Stearns Davis*	198
ANTONY'S ADDRESS TO THE ROMANS ON THE DEATH OF CÆSAR (from "Julius Cæsar") . . . . . *William Shakespeare*	211
THE ROMAN FORUM (from "Stories in Stone from the Roman Forum") . . . . *Isabel Lovell*	221
THE GOLDEN MILE-STONE . . *Henry Wadsworth Longfellow*	224
THE COLOSSEUM (from "Pictures from Italy") *Charles Dickens*	226
ANDROCLUS AND THE LION	229
THE BAY OF NAPLES	233
DRIFTING . . . . *Thomas Buchanan Read*	236
THE HOUSE OF GLAUCUS (from "The Last Days of Pompeii") *Bulwer-Lytton*	238
GAINING WINGS . . . . *Edna Dean Proctor*	242
THE BLIND FLOWER GIRL (from "The Last Days of Pompeii") *Bulwer-Lytton*	244
THE BOY AND THE ANGEL . . . . . . *Robert Browning*	248
THE ERUPTION OF VESUVIUS (from "The Last Days of Pompeii") *Bulwer-Lytton*	253
HOW PLINY SAVED HIS MOTHER (from the Letter of Pliny the Younger to Tacitus)	261
THE CHAMBERED NAUTILUS . . . *Oliver Wendell Holmes*	264
THE EXCAVATIONS AT POMPEII	266
SELECTIONS FROM MARCUS AURELIUS	270
MY BOOKS . . . . *Justin Huntly McCarthy*	276

ILLUSTRATIONS

EGYPT

	PAGE
The Obelisk of Heliopolis	Frontispiece
Father Nile. *After the statue in the Vatican*	3
The Road to the Pyramids	7
The Pyramids and the Nile	8
The Sphinx	9
The Sphinx and the Great Pyramid	10
Napoleon before the Sphinx. *After the painting by J. L. Gérôme*	13
Gizeh	14
A Prayer in the Desert. *After the painting by Horace Vernet*	16
Pylon at Karnak	19
Statue of Rameses II	20
In the Hall of Columns, Temple of Ammon, Karnak	21
The Land of Egypt	33
A Temple in Nubia	34
A Mosque in Cairo	55
An Arabian Sheik	58
An Arabian Village on the Banks of the Nile	59
A Moorish Shop	60
Avenue of Sphinxes at Karnak	63
Boats on the Nile	65
The Statues of Memnon	69
Colonnade of the Temple of Edfu, Upper Egypt	71
Antony and Cleopatra. *After the painting by Alma-Tadema*	79
Pillars at Karnak	85
Kiosk at Philae	88

GREECE

The Mourning Athena	92
Gods from the Parthenon Frieze	99
Caryatid Porch in Erechtheum	103
A Reading from Homer. *After the painting by Alma-Tadema*	108
The Theseum	119
Young Horsemen, from the Parthenon Frieze	120

WORLD LITERATURE READERS

	PAGE
The Wingèd Victory of Samothrace	124
Greek Costumes. *After the painting by J. Coomans*	127
Mercury. *From the statue by Giovanni da Bologna*	137
Jupiter. *After a bust in the Vatican*	142
North Porch of the Erechtheum	152
Mount Lycabettus from the Parthenon	156
Front of the Parthenon	158
The Approach to the Acropolis	161
The Acropolis restored	163
The Hermes of Praxiteles. *After the statue at Olympia*	165
The Acropolis and the Temple of Jupiter	175
Greek Girls playing Ball. *After the painting by Sir Frederick Leighton*	176

ROME

Ancient Italy. *After the painting by J. M. W. Turner*	178
The Flight of Æneas. *After the painting by Raphael*	183
The Cumæan Sibyl. *After the painting by Elihu Vedder*	186
Ruins of the Temple of Castor and Pollux	191
Temple of Vesta in Rome	195
The Appian Way in Cæsar's Time	209
Julius Cæsar	215
Ruins of the Roman Forum	222
The Appian Way	223
Ruins of the House of the Vestals, Roman Forum	225
The Arch of Constantine	227
The Colosseum	228
The Bay of Naples and Vesuvius	233
The Blue Grotto, Capri	234
Capri	237
A Pompeian Courtyard	239
The Vestal Tuccia. *After the painting by Hector Le Roux*	243
Nydia. *After the painting by Bodenhausen*	245
A Roman Mother and Daughter. *After the painting by J. Coomans*	247
Angel with Viola. *After the painting by Melozzo da Forlì*	251
Pompeii and Vesuvius	255
Eruption of Vesuvius in 1872	256
The House of Pansa, Pompeii	267
A Street in Pompeii	268
The Tiber and the Castle of St. Angelo	271
Marcus Aurelius	273
Pyramid of Cestius in Rome	275

THE OBELISK OF HELIOPOLIS

EGYPT

THE RIVER NILE[1]

WALTER SCOTT PERRY

Little wonder that to the ancient Egyptians the river Nile was a mystery they regarded with a feeling of reverence, believing that a god dwelt within its waters. For many hundred miles from the mouth no tributary breaks its winding outline. Onward it flows through rainless regions, beneath an almost tropical sun, spreading abroad the fertile bounty which for untold centuries made Egypt the granary of the world. Tens of thousands of people still dwell upon its productive banks, drawing daily from its fountain of waters for purposes of irrigation and domestic consumption. Seemingly the river grows wider and deeper as it makes its way toward the Mediterranean, although it actually loses one third of its volume. Every year, beginning in June, it slowly

[1] Copyright, 1898, by The Prang Educational Company. Used by special permission.

fills its bed between the steep alluvial banks, and then as deliberately spreads its turbid waters over the rich soil to the desert's edge. Having deposited its freight of vitalized earth, its mission accomplished, it gradually recedes and, reaching its winding bed, again sinks many feet below the level surface of the land.

The annual overflow of the Nile no longer turns its valley into a great lake, as it must have done in earlier times, for, through engineering skill, man now controls to a certain extent the waters of the river. By means of canals these waters are conducted to supply somewhat remote districts during the dry season.

The productive soil left by the retreating Nile requires but the merest scratching of its yielding surface by the primitive plow to be made ready for the seed. Owing, however, to the absence of rain, the crops must be watered continually by artificial means; therefore, throughout the long days, hundreds of native workmen draw water from the river and raise it to the little canals which, like the lines of a checkerboard, divide the arable land.

The water is lifted from the river by means of a shadoof. This rude apparatus consists of a long pole, like a well sweep, with a bucket at one end and a ball of dried mud as a weight at the other. When

EGYPT

the river is low, a man stationed at the water's edge fills the bucket, raises it with his shadoof, and pours the water into a hole in the embankment above him. Other men above, each with a shadoof, successively dip and lift the water upward until the top of the embankment is reached. By a network of little canals the water is conducted over a tract of cultivated soil.

FATHER NILE
After the statue in the Vatican

Week after week this operation is repeated, furnishing employment to many men, who receive from ten to fifteen cents per day for their labor.

The life along the river is unique and interesting. Flat-bottomed boats, freighted with merchandise brought by camels across the desert to Assuan, float down the river, their sails, like the wings of gigantic birds, sharply outlined against the clear sky. Here and there along the banks may be seen women filling their water jars.

No day in the Egyptian country closes without a glorious sunset. The great ball of fire drops into the sand of the Libyan desert; the river becomes a field of magnificent color; palm groves are silhouetted against the sky; strange outlines are seen here and there; the women go to the river to fill their water jars; weird forms hurry to and fro; then suddenly the wonderful afterglow streams up from the western horizon. The heavens become a play of color. It is like a glorious transformation from the realities of life into the ideal surroundings of another world, beautiful beyond description. Then the color fades away; darkness comes rapidly; it is night, and all is quiet upon the dark shores of the river Nile.

Abridged from " Egypt, the Land of
the Temple Builders "

Heliopolis (hē lĭ ŏp'ō lĭs). — **shadoof** (shä dōōf'). — **Vatican**: the Pope's palace, adjoining the church of St. Peter in Rome. — **Assuan** (äs swän'). — **Libyan** (lĭb'ĭ an). — **silhouetted** (sĭl'ōō ĕt'ĕd): projected upon a background, so that the outlines of an object are filled in with a black or a dark, uniform color.

THE PYRAMIDS AND THE SPHINX

George William Curtis

Upon the chaotic desert that tumbles eastward from an infinite horizon, jagged in sandy billows that seem to be falling back upon themselves, rose the pyramids — dumb, inexplicable forms; dimmest and farthest of all, the great pyramids of Gizeh, looming in the faint haze of noon, like the relics of fore-world art, defying curiosity and speculation.

We slipped down to Gizeh and early the next morning donkeyed quietly to the pyramids. Except for the sake of the sphinx the howadji would advise the visit only to the scientific and curious, and is the more willing to say so because he knows that every traveler would not fail to go. But the pyramids were built for the distant eye, and their poetic grandeur and charm belong to distance. When your eye first strikes them, as you come up from Alexandria to Cairo, they stand out, vague, rosy, and distant, and are at once and entirely the Egypt of your dreams. The river winds and winds, and they seem to shift their places, to be now here, now there, now on the western shore, now on the eastern, until Egypt becomes, to your only too glowing fancy, a bright day and a pyramid.

Walk out beyond the village of Gizeh at twilight, then, and see them, not nearer than the breadth of the plain. They will seem to gather up the whole world into silence, and you will feel a pathos in their dumbness quite below your tears. They have outlived speech, and are no more intelligible. Yet the freshness of youth still flushes in the sunset along their sides, and even these severe and awful forms have a beautiful bloom, as of Hesperidian fruit, in your memory and imagination.

But as you approach they shrink and shrink, and when you stand at their bases and cast your eye to the apex, they are but vast mountains of masonry, sloping upward to the sky. Bedouins, importunate for endless baksheesh, will pull you, breathless and angry, to the summit, and promise to run up and over all possible pyramids and, for aught you know, throw you across to the peaks of their Sakkara cousins. Only threats most terrible and entirely impossible of performance can restore the necessary silence. Express distinctly your determination to plunge every Bedouin down the pyramid, when they have you, dizzy and breathless and gasping, on the sides, as you go up from layer to layer, like stairs; swear in your gasping and rage that you will only begin by throwing them down, but will conclude by annihilating the whole tribe who haunt the pyramids

THE ROAD TO THE PYRAMIDS

— and you work a miracle, for the Bedouins become as placidly silent as if your threats were feasible, and only mutter mildly, " Baksheesh, howadji," like retiring and innocent thunder.

There are those who explore the pyramids — who, from poetic or other motives, go into an utterly dark,

THE PYRAMIDS AND THE NILE

hot, and noisome interior, see a broken sarcophagus, feel that they are incased in solid masonry, hear the howls of Bedouins, and return faint, exhausted, smoke-blackened, with their pockets picked and their nerves direfully disturbed. To such the exploration of the pyramids may be as it was to Nero —

a grand and memorable epoch in his life, for he said that he felt the greatness of old Egypt more profoundly in the pyramids than anywhere else.

Yet you must seek the pyramids, else you would miss the sphinx, and the memory of that omission would more sadly haunt you afterwards than her riddle haunted the old victims of her spells.

THE SPHINX

The desert is enamored of his grotesque darling, and gradually gathers around it and draws it back again to his bosom. It well seems the child of desert inspiration. It lies on the very edge of the desert, which recoils above the plain as at Sakkara. The sand has covered it, and only head, neck, and back are above its level. In vain Caviglia strove to stay the desert. More than half of the sand that he daily excavated blew back again at night.

The sphinx, with raised head, gazes expectantly toward the east, nor dropped its eyes when Cambyses or Napoleon came. The nose is gone and the lips are gradually going; the constant attrition of

THE SPHINX AND THE GREAT PYRAMID

sand grains wears them away. The back is a mass of rock, and the temple between the forepaws is buried forever. " Still unread is my riddle," it seems to say, and looks untiring for him who shall solve it. Its beauty is more Nubian than Egyptian, or is rather a blending of both. Its bland gaze is serious and sweet. Yet unwinking, unbending, in the yellow moonlight silence of those desert sands, will it breathe mysteries more magical, and rarer romances of the

EGYPT

Mountains of the Moon and the Nile sources than ever Arabian imagination dreamed. Be glad that the sphinx was your last wonder upon the Nile, for it seems to contain and express the rest. And from its thinned and thinning lips, as you move back to the river with all Egypt behind you, trails a voice inaudible, like a serpent gorgeously folding about your memory—" Egypt and mystery, O sphinx!"

Adapted from " Nile Notes of a Howadji "

Sphinx (sfĭnks). — **Gizeh** (gē′zĕ). — **howadji** (hou äj′ĭ): a traveler or merchant. In early times the travelers were merchants. — **Cairo** (kī′rō). — **Hesperidian** (hĕs pēr ĭd′ĭ an) **fruit**: fabled golden apples of Hesperides (hĕs pĕr′ĭ dēz), supposed to grow in western Africa, carried away by Hercules (hẽr′cŭ lēz), who slew the dragon that guarded the fruit. — **Bedouins** (bĕd′ōō ĭnz): Arabs who live in tents and who are scattered over Arabia, Egypt, and other parts of Africa. — **baksheesh** (băk′shĕsh): a present of money. — **Sakkara** (säk kä′rä): a village near Memphis in Egypt, containing one of the oldest pyramids and a famous avenue of sphinxes. — **Nero** (nē′rŏ): a Roman emperor, cruel and tyrannical. — **riddle of the sphinx**: referring to an old tradition that the sphinx put to death all who could not answer this question: "What is it that has first four feet, then two, and finally three?" Œdipus (ĕd′ĭ pus), a Greek, answered that it is man, who creeps in infancy and goes with a staff in old age. — **Caviglia** (cä vē′yĕ a): an Italian who attempted to excavate the body of the sphinx. — **Cambyses** (căm bī′sēz): a famous Persian king who conquered Egypt in 527 B.C. — **Napoleon** (na pō′lĕ un): the great French general and conqueror, who fought with most of the nations of Europe. His expedition to Egypt was a failure. He was overthrown by the English at Waterloo in Belgium, and imprisoned on the island of St. Helena (hĕ lē′na) for the remainder of his life. — **Nubian** (nū′bĭ an): from Nubia, a country south of Egypt. The Nubians were a very handsome people with black skins; they were tall and well-proportioned. — **Mountains of the Moon**: once supposed to be in the interior of Africa. They have disappeared from the map.

THE SPHINX SPEAKS

Francis Saltus Saltus

Carved by a mighty race whose vanished hands
Formed empires more destructible than I,
In sultry silence I forever lie,
Wrapped in the shifting garment of the sands.
Below me Pharaoh's scintillating bands
With clashings of loud cymbals have passed by,
And the eternal reverence of the sky
Falls royally on me and all my lands.

The record of the future broods in me;
I have with worlds of blazing stars been crowned,
But none my subtle mystery hath known
Save one, who made his way through blood and sea,
The Corsican, prophetic and renowned,
To whom I spake, one awful night alone!

    Pharaoh (fā'rō): a title of the kings of ancient Egypt. — **the Corsican** (kôr'sĭ can): Napoleon, who was born on the island of Corsica. — **Gérôme** (zhā rōm').

NAPOLEON BEFORE THE SPHINX
After the painting by J. L. Gérôme

GIZEH
The edge of the desert

THE APPROACH TO THE DESERT

Robert Smythe Hichens

From the railway carriage they watched the great change that was coming over the land.

It seemed as if God were putting forth his hand to withdraw gradually all things of his creation, — all the furniture he has put into the great palace of the world, — as if he meant to leave it empty and naked.

First he took the rich and shaggy grass and all the little flowers that bloomed modestly in it. Then he drew away the orange groves, the oleander and the apricot trees, the sweet waters that fertilized the soil, the tufted plants and giant reeds that crowd where water is. And still, as the train ran on, his gifts were fewer. At last even the palms were gone, and the Barbary fig displayed no longer its tortured strength and the fantastic evolutions of its foliage. Stones lay everywhere upon the pale-yellow or gray-brown earth. Crystals glittered in the sun like shallow jewels, and far away appeared hard and relentless mountains which looked as if they were made of iron.

Journeying toward those terrible fastnesses were caravans, moving slowly toward their rock villages.

Over the withered earth they went toward the distant mountains. The wind continued to rise. Sand

A PRAYER IN THE DESERT
After the painting by Horace Vernet

found its way in through the carriage windows. The desolation of the country had become so absolute that one could not conceive of anything but still greater desolation lying beyond. One seemed to have passed the boundary of the world God had created, and come into some other place, upon which he had never looked.

There were no Arabs journeying now, no tents huddled among the low bushes. The last sign of vegetation was obliterated. The earth rose and fell in a series of humps and depressions. Every shade of yellow and of brown mingled and flowed away toward the foot of the mountains. Here and there dry watercourses showed their teeth. Their crumbling banks were like the rind of an orange. Little birds, the hue of the earth, with tufted crests, tripped jauntily among the stones, fluttered for a few yards, and alighted with an air of strained alertness, as if their minute bodies were full of trembling wires. They were the only living things to be seen.

The wind was really cold and was blowing gustily. There was a wonderful, a startling flavor in it — the flavor of gigantic spaces and of rolling leagues of emptiness. Neither among mountains nor upon the sea had one ever found an atmosphere so fiercely pure, clean, and lively with unutterable freedom.

Barbary fig: the prickly pear, a sort of cactus. — **Vernet** (vĕr nā´).

THE TEMPLE OF KARNAK[1]

Walter Scott Perry

How glorious was ancient Thebes when the great kings of the eighteenth and nineteenth dynasties ruled in Upper Egypt, when the greatest temples the world has ever seen — the temples of Karnak and of Luxor — had been erected upon the eastern bank of the Nile, and when processions of priests wended their way through the city and between rows of silent sphinxes to the temple gates!

The gigantic temple of Karnak has been called the wonder of the ages. Its fame became known to the ancient Persians and to the Greeks. More than thirty centuries divide the past of Karnak from the life of to-day; yet still delicate are the carvings, brilliant is the coloring of ornament, wonderful are the cuttings of the hieroglyphic language, which tell us how man has lived and worshiped and how the web of life has been woven during this long period of time.

About a mile and a half from Luxor are the ruins of Karnak. Not one temple, but many temples; not one pylon, or gateway, but many pylons,

[1] Copyright, 1898, by The Prang Educational Company. Used by special permission.

EGYPT

PYLON AT KARNAK

mark the site of monuments the very ruins of which are the grandest in the world. One travels across the fields along an embankment of earth until he reaches the ancient processional roadway, which is still beautiful with its arching palm trees and its fragments of sculptured sphinxes.

The temple of Chunsu is the one usually spoken of as "the temple of Karnak," though it is only one of many. This temple was erected by Rameses III in honor of Chunsu, the son of Ammon, the Theban god. In an inscription found on a papyrus roll Rameses is represented as saying, "I built a house in Thebes for thy son Chunsu, of good hewn stone, its doors covered with gold adorned with electrum like the celestial horizon."

STATUE OF RAMESES II

The largest of the Karnak temples is the temple of Ammon. The immense portal — three hundred and seventy-two feet wide, one hundred and forty-two feet high, and sixteen feet thick — faces the Nile. The remains of an avenue of sphinxes stretch from the temple to

IN THE HALL OF COLUMNS
Ruins of the Temple of Ammon at Karnak

the river. In imagination we go back to the time of ancient pageantries, when the king and priests and devout men paid tribute to their gods. We picture the gayety of the scene, — the state barges, with decorations in gold and brilliant color, sailing slowly up the Nile, greeted by choirs upon the river bank singing praise songs to the great Ammon. We can see the boats draw up one by one at the landing place, from them passing priests and dignitaries, whose jeweled gowns sparkle in the bright sun. Finally the procession, led by the king and the high priest, is formed. Slowly it wends its way toward the temple, spreading itself like a gay oriental carpet at the feet of the couchant sphinxes, while above the pylon float the colors of Upper and Lower Egypt.

The first great court of the temple measured three hundred and thirty-eight feet in width by two hundred and seventy-five feet in depth. The great pylon formed its portal, while at the other end of the court a second pylon framed the entrance to that wonderful Hall of Columns, the marvel of the ages. The broad central passageway is formed by a double row of columns measuring seventy feet in height. The shafts of the columns are nearly twelve feet in diameter and thirty-six feet in circumference. The capitals are eleven feet in height, and their enormous corolla-shaped tops spread out as if to support the very dome of heaven.

EGYPT

Who can describe this forest of columns — their prodigious size and the power displayed in their construction? Their shafts still chronicle deeds of men of princely power. Why built they on a scale so vast? Was it to fulfill their conceptions of a spiritual life?

The mystery of worship that caused the erection of these temples still pervades the pillared halls. The great stones seem cemented with the lifeblood of a bonded people, who, though unknown to the world to-day, have left the imprints of human life upon these colossal, time-defying monuments.

Adapted from " Egypt, the Land of the Temple Builders "

Karnak (kär'nák). — **Thebes** (thēbz): a ruined city in Upper Egypt. — **eighteenth and nineteenth dynasties** (dī'nas tĭz): in Egyptian history, about 1600–1200 B.C. The kings of these two dynasties, or families, are said to have been the greatest race of kings that ever reigned upon the earth, and they made Egypt a great power. Rameses II belonged to the nineteenth dynasty. — **Luxor** (lŭk'sôr): a village near the site of ancient Thebes. — **pylon** (pī'lŏn). — **Chunsu** (kōōn'sōō). — **Rameses** (răm'ē sēz). — **electrum** (ĕ lĕk'trŭm): an alloy of silver and gold, the color of amber. — **couchant** (kouch'ạnt): lying down with head upraised. — **capitals**: the uppermost parts of columns or pillars.

ABOU BEN ADHEM

Leigh Hunt

Abou Ben Adhem (may his tribe increase!)
Awoke one night from a deep dream of peace,
And saw, within the moonlight in his room,
Making it rich, and like a lily in bloom,
An angel writing in a book of gold:—
Exceeding peace had made Ben Adhem bold,
And to the presence in the room he said,
"What writest thou?"—The vision raised its head,
And with a look made of all sweet accord,
Answered, "The names of those who love the Lord."
"And is mine one?" said Abou. "Nay, not so,"
Replied the angel. Abou spoke more low,
But cheerly still; and said, "I pray thee then,
Write me as one that loves his fellow-men."

The angel wrote, and vanished. The next night
It came again with a great wakening light,
And showed the names whom love of God had blessed,
And lo! Ben Adhem's name led all the rest.

Abou Ben Adhem (ä′bōō běn ä′děm). — **may his tribe increase**: it is customary in Arabic literature to throw in such a phrase of blessing after mentioning the name of a saint.

THE STORY OF JOSEPH

Now Jacob loved Joseph more than all his children, because he was the son of his old age, and he made him a coat of many colors. And when his brethren saw that their father loved him more than all his brethren, they hated him and could not speak peaceably unto him.

And Joseph dreamed a dream, and he told it to his brethren, and they hated him yet the more. And he said unto them, "Hear, I pray you, this dream which I have dreamed: Behold, we were binding sheaves in the field, and lo, my sheaf arose and also stood upright; and behold, your sheaves stood round about and made obeisance to my sheaf."

And his brethren said unto him, "Shalt thou indeed reign over us? or shalt thou indeed have dominion over us?" And they hated him yet the more for his dreams and for his words.

And he dreamed yet another dream and told it to his brethren and said, "Behold, I have dreamed a dream more; and behold, the sun and the moon and the eleven stars made obeisance to me."

And he told it to his father and to his brethren, and his father rebuked him and said unto him: "What is this dream that thou hast dreamed? Shall

I and thy mother and thy brethren indeed come to bow down ourselves to thee to the earth?" And his brethren envied him, but his father observed the saying.

And his brethren went to feed their father's flock in Shechem. And Jacob said unto Joseph: "Do not thy brethren feed the flock in Shechem? Come, and I will send thee unto them."

And he said to him, "Here am I."

And he said to him, "Go, I pray thee, see whether it be well with thy brethren, and well with the flocks; and bring me word again."

So he sent him out of the vale of Hebron, and he came to Shechem. And a certain man found him, and behold, he was wandering in the field, and the man asked him, saying, "What seekest thou?"

And he said, "I seek my brethren; tell me, I pray thee, where they feed their flocks."

And the man said, "They are departed hence, for I heard them say, 'Let us go to Dothan.'"

And Joseph went after his brethren and found them in Dothan. And when they saw him afar off, even before he came near unto them, they conspired against him to slay him. And they said one to another: "Behold, this dreamer cometh. Come now, therefore, and let us slay him, and cast him into some pit, and we will say some evil beast hath devoured him, and we shall see what will become of his dreams."

And Reuben heard it, and he delivered him out of their hands and said, "Let us not kill him, but cast him into this pit that is in the wilderness, and lay no hand upon him," that he might rid him out of their hands, to deliver him to his father again.

And it came to pass, when Joseph was come unto his brethren, that they stripped Joseph out of his coat of many colors, and they took him and cast him into a pit.

And they sat down to eat bread, and they lifted up their eyes and looked, and behold, a company of Ishmaelites came from Gilead with their camels, bearing spicery and balm and myrrh, going to carry it down to Egypt.

And Judah said unto his brethren: "What profit is it if we slay our brother and conceal his blood? Come, and let us sell him to the Ishmaelites, and let not our hand be upon him, for he is our brother and our flesh." And his brethren were content.

Then there passed by Midianites, merchantmen; and his brethren drew and lifted up Joseph out of the pit and sold him to the Ishmaelites for twenty pieces of silver, and they brought Joseph into Egypt.

And Reuben returned unto the pit, and behold, Joseph was not in the pit, and he rent his clothes.

And he returned unto his brethren and said, "The child is not, and I, whither shall I go?"

And they took Joseph's coat and killed a kid of the goats and dipped the coat in the blood, and they sent the coat of many colors, and they brought it to their father and said, "This have we found; know now whether it be thy son's coat or no."

And he knew it and said, "It is my son's coat; an evil beast hath devoured him; Joseph is without doubt rent in pieces."

And Jacob rent his clothes and put sackcloth upon his loins and mourned for his son many days.

And all his sons and all his daughters rose up to comfort him, but he refused to be comforted, and he said, "I will go down into the grave unto my son mourning." Thus his father wept for him.

And the Midianites sold him into Egypt unto Potiphar, an officer of Pharaoh's and captain of the guard.

And the Lord was with Joseph, and he was a prosperous man, and he was in the house of his master the Egyptian.

And his master saw that the Lord was with him, and that the Lord made all that he did to prosper in his hand. And Joseph found grace in his sight, and he served him, and he made him overseer over his house, and all that he had he put into his hand. And the Lord blessed the Egyptian's house for Joseph's sake.

. . . .

And it came to pass that Pharaoh dreamed and that his spirit was troubled, and he sent and called for all the magicians of Egypt and all the wise men thereof, and Pharaoh told them his dreams, but there was none that could interpret them unto Pharaoh.

Then Pharaoh sent and called Joseph. And Pharaoh said unto Joseph, "I have dreamed a dream, and there is none that can interpret it, and I have heard say of thee that thou canst understand a dream to interpret it."

And Joseph answered Pharaoh, saying, "It is not in me; God shall give Pharaoh an answer of peace."

And Pharaoh said unto Joseph, "In my dream, behold, I stood upon the bank of a river; and behold, there came up out of the river seven kine, fat-fleshed and well-favored, and they fed in a meadow; and behold, seven other kine came up after them, poor and very ill-favored and lean-fleshed, such as I never saw in all the land of Egypt for badness; and the lean and ill-favored kine did eat up the first seven fat kine; and when they had eaten them up, it could not be known that they had eaten them; but they were still ill-favored, as at the beginning. So I awoke.

"And I saw in my dream, and behold, seven ears

came up in one stalk, full and good; and behold, seven ears, withered, thin, and blasted with the east wind, sprang up after them; and the thin ears devoured the seven good ears; and I told this unto the magicians, but there was none that could declare it unto me."

And Joseph said unto Pharaoh: "The dream of Pharaoh is one; God hath showed Pharaoh what he is about to do. The seven good kine are seven years; and the seven good ears are seven years; the dream is one. And the seven thin and ill-favored kine that came up after them are seven years; and the seven empty ears blasted with the east wind shall be seven years of famine. Behold, there come seven years of great plenty throughout all the land of Egypt, and there shall arise after them seven years of famine, and all the years of plenty shall be forgotten in the land of Egypt, and the famine shall consume the land. Now therefore let Pharaoh look out a man discreet and wise, and set him over the land of Egypt. Let Pharaoh do this and let him appoint officers over the land and take up the fifth part of the land of Egypt in the seven plenteous years. And let them gather all the food of those good years, and lay up corn under the hand of Pharaoh, and let them keep food in the cities. And that food shall be for store in the land against the seven years of famine."

EGYPT

And the thing was good in the eyes of Pharaoh and in the eyes of all his servants. And Pharaoh said unto Joseph: "Forasmuch as God hath showed thee all this, there is none so discreet and wise as thou art. Thou shalt be over my house, and according unto thy word shall all my people be ruled; only in the throne will I be greater than thou." And Pharaoh took off his ring from his hand and put it upon Joseph's hand and arrayed him in vestures of fine linen and put a gold chain about his neck; and he made him to ride in the second chariot which he had, and they cried before him, "Bow the knee!" And he made him ruler over all the land of Egypt.

And Joseph went throughout all the land of Egypt. And in the seven plenteous years the earth brought forth by handfuls. And he gathered up all the food of the seven years and laid up the food in the cities.

And the seven years of plenteousness were ended. And the seven years of dearth began to come, and the dearth was in all lands, but in all the land of Egypt there was bread.

And all countries came into Egypt to Joseph to buy corn, because the famine was so sore in all lands. And Joseph's brethren went down to buy corn in Egypt. And Joseph was the governor over the land, and Joseph's brethren came and bowed down themselves before him with their faces to the earth.

Then Joseph could not refrain himself before all them that stood by him, and he cried, "Cause every man to go out from me."

And there stood no man with him while Joseph made himself known unto his brethren. And he wept aloud. And Joseph said unto his brethren, "I am Joseph; doth my father yet live?"

And his brethren could not answer him, for they were troubled at his presence.

And Joseph said unto his brethren: "Come near to me, I pray you. I am Joseph, your brother, whom ye sold into Egypt. Now, therefore, be not grieved, nor be angry with yourselves, that ye sold me hither, for God did send me before you to preserve you, and to save your lives by a great deliverance. So now, it was not you that sent me hither, but God; and he hath made me a father to Pharaoh, and lord of all his house, and a ruler throughout all the land of Egypt. Haste ye and go up to my father and say unto him, 'Thus saith thy son Joseph, "God hath made me lord of all Egypt; come down unto me; tarry not; and thou shalt dwell in the land of Goshen, and thou shalt be near unto me,— thou, and thy children, and thy children's children, and thy flocks, and thy herds, and all that thou hast; and there will I nourish thee, — for there are yet five years of famine,— lest thou, and thy household, and all that

EGYPT

THE LAND OF EGYPT

thou hast come to poverty."' And ye shall haste and bring down my father hither."

So he sent his brethren away, and they went up out of Egypt and came into the land of Canaan unto Jacob their father, and told him, saying, "Joseph is yet alive, and he is governor over all the land of Egypt." And they told him all the words of Joseph.

And Jacob said, "It is enough; Joseph my son is yet alive; I will go and see him before I die."

Adapted from Genesis xxxvii–xlv

Shechem (shē′kĕm): an ancient city of Palestine. — **Hebron** (hē′brŭn): an ancient city of southern Palestine. — **Dothan** (dō′thạn): a town of Palestine, about twelve miles north of Samaria. — **Ishmaelites** (ĭsh′mȧ ĕl ĭts): a wandering tribe of the desert, the descendants of Ishmael (ĭsh′mȧ ĕl), the son of Abraham and Hagar (hā′gạr). — **Midianites** (mĭd′ĭ ạn īts): a wandering tribe, also descendants of Abraham; here used interchangeably with *Ishmaelites*. — **Potiphar** (pŏt′ĭ fạr). — **Goshen** (gō′shĕn): a grazing region near the mouth of the Nile. — **Canaan** (cā′nạn): an ancient name for Palestine.

THE SEVENTH PLAGUE OF EGYPT

George Croly

See Exodus iii–xiii for the story of the ten plagues of Egypt, and of the final escape of the Israelites from bondage.

'T was morn, the rising splendor rolled
On marble towers and roofs of gold;
Hall, court, and gallery below
Were crowded with a living flow,
Egyptian, Arab, Nubian, there,—
The bearers of the bow and spear,
The hoary priest, the Chaldee sage,
The slave, the gemmed and glittering page,—
Helm, turban, and tiara shone
A dazzling ring round Pharaoh's throne.

There came a man[1]— the human tide
Shrank backward from his stately stride;
His cheek with storm and time was tanned,
A shepherd's staff was in his hand;
A shudder of instinctive fear
Told the dark king what step was near.
On through the host the stranger came,
It parted round his form like flame.

[1] Moses.

He stooped not at the footstool stone,
He clasped not sandal, kissed not throne;
Erect he stood amid the ring,
His only words, " Be just, O king! "
On Pharaoh's cheek the blood flushed high,
A fire was in his sullen eye,
Yet on the chief of Israel
No arrow of his thousands fell;
All mute and moveless as the grave
Stood chilled the satrap and the slave.

" Thou 'rt come," at length the monarch spoke
(Haughty and high the words outbroke);
" Is Israel weary of its lair,
The forehead peeled, the shoulder bare?
Take back the answer to your band:
'Go, reap the wind! Go, plow the sand!
Go, vilest of the living vile,
To build the never-ending pile!
What better asks the howling slave
Than the base life our bounty gave?'"

" King, thou and thine are doomed! Behold! "
The prophet spoke — the thunder rolled!
Along the pathway of the sun
Sailed vapory mountains, wild and dun.
" Yet there is time," the prophet said;
He raised his staff — the storm was stayed;

EGYPT

" King, be the word of freedom given!
What art thou, man, to war with Heaven? "

There came no word — the thunder broke!
Like a huge city's final smoke,
Thick, lurid, stifling, mixed with flame,
Through court and hall the vapors came.
Loose as the stubble in the field
Wide flew the men of spear and shield;
Scattered like foam along the wave
Flew the proud pageant, prince, and slave.
" Speak, king! the wrath is but begun!
Still dumb? Then, Heaven, thy will be done! "

Echoed from earth a hollow roar
Like ocean on the midnight shore;
A sheet of lightning o'er them wheeled,
The solid ground beneath them reeled;
In dust sank roof and battlement,
Like webs the giant walls were rent;
Red, broad, before his startled gaze
The monarch saw his Egypt blaze.
Still swelled the plague — the flame grew pale,
Burst from the clouds the charge of hail.

Still swelled the plague — uprose the blast,
The avenger, fit to be the last.

On ocean, river, forest, vale,
Thundered at once the mighty gale;
Before the whirlwind flew the tree,
Beneath the whirlwind roared the sea;
A thousand ships were on the wave —
Where are they? Ask that foaming grave!

And lo! that first fierce triumph o'er,
Swells ocean on the shrinking shore,
Still onward, onward, dark and wide,
Engulfs the land the furious tide.
Then bowed thy spirit, stubborn king,
Thou serpent, reft of fang and sting;
Humbled before the prophet's knee
He groaned, " Be injured Israel free!"

To heaven the sage upraised his hand —
Back rolled the deluge from the land,
Back to its caverns sank the gale,
Fled from the noon the vapors pale;
Broad burned again the joyous sun,
The hour of wrath and death was done.

seventh plague: see Exodus ix, 13-35. — **Israelites** (ĭz′rȧ ĕl īts): descendants of Israel, a name given to Jacob. — **Chaldee** (kăl′dē) **sage**: a wise man of Chaldea (kăl dē′ȧ). — **helm**: helmet. — **tiara** (tĭ ā′rȧ): a head-dress worn by the ancient Persians, resembling a hat with a high crown. — **satrap** (sā′trăp): the governor of a province. — **The forehead peeled**: they probably carried packs by means of a leathern strap passed over the forehead. — **To build the never-ending pile**: the Israelites formed part of the horde of slaves who erected the temples and pyramids of Egypt.

THE FISHERMAN AND THE GENIE

There was a very ancient fisherman, so poor that he could scarcely earn enough to maintain himself, his wife, and his three children. He went every day to fish betimes in the morning, and imposed it as a law upon himself not to cast his nets more than four times a day. He went one morning by moonlight, and coming to the seaside cast in his nets. As he drew them toward the shore he found them very heavy and thought he had a good draft of fish, at which he rejoiced within himself; but a moment after he found there was nothing in the nets but a basket of gravel and slime, which grieved him exceedingly. He threw away the basket, and washing his nets from the slime, he cast them in the second time, but brought up nothing except stone, shells, and mud. Almost beside himself with despair he cast the nets the third time, and with the same result. However, when daylight appeared, he did not forget to say his prayers, like a good Mussulman.

The fisherman, having finished his prayers, cast his nets the fourth time, and when he thought they might he filled, he drew them, as formerly, with great difficulty, but instead of fish he found nothing in them but a vessel of yellow copper, which, by its weight, seemed to be full of something. He observed that it was shut up and sealed with lead, having the impression of a seal upon it. This rejoiced him.

"I will sell it," said he, "and with the money arising from it buy a measure of corn."

He examined the vessel on all sides and shook it to see if what was within made any noise, but heard nothing. This circumstance, with the impression of the seal upon the leaden cover, made him think there was something precious in it. He took a knife and opened the jar with very little labor. He presently turned the mouth downward, but nothing came out. He set it before him, and while he looked upon it attentively, there issued a very thick smoke, which obliged him to retire two or three paces. The smoke ascended to the clouds and, extending itself along the sea and upon the shore, formed a great mist which did mightily astonish the fisherman. When the smoke was all out of the vessel, it reunited itself and became a solid body, of which there was formed a genie twice as high as the greatest of giants. At this sight the fisherman would fain have fled, but he was so frightened he could not go one step.

"Solomon!" cried the genie immediately,— "Solomon, the great prophet,— pardon, pardon! I will never more oppose your will; I will obey all your commands."

The fisherman, when he heard these words from the genie, recovered his courage and said to him: "Proud spirit, what is it that you say? It is above eighteen hundred years since the prophet Solomon died, and we are now at the end of time. Tell me your history, and how you came to be shut up in this vessel."

The genie, turning to the fisherman with a fierce look, said, "You must speak to me with more civility; you are very bold to call me a proud spirit."

"Very well," replied the fisherman, "shall I call you the owl of good luck?"

"I say," answered the genie, "speak to me more civilly before I kill you."

"Ah!" replied the fisherman, "why should you kill me? Did I not just now set you at liberty, and have you already forgotten it?"

"Yes, I remember it," said the genie, "but that shall not prevent me from killing you. I have only one favor to grant you."

"And what is that?" said the fisherman.

"It is," answered the genie, "to give you your choice in what manner you would have me take your life."

"But wherein have I offended you?" replied the fisherman. "Is that your reward for the good services I have done you?"

"I cannot treat you otherwise," said the genie, "and that you may be convinced of it, hearken to my story. I am one of those rebellious spirits that opposed Solomon, the great prophet, and submitted not to him. The great monarch sent Asaph, his chief minister, to apprehend me. That was accordingly done. Asaph seized my person and brought me by force before his master's throne.

"Solomon, the son of David, commanded me to quit my way of living, to acknowledge his power, and to submit myself to his command. I bravely refused to obey, and told him I would rather expose myself to his resentment than swear fealty and submit to him as he required. To punish me, he shut me up in this copper vessel, and gave it to one of the genii who submitted to him, with orders to throw me into the sea, which order was executed, to my sorrow. During the first hundred years of imprisonment I swore that if any one would deliver me before the hundred years expired, I would make him rich beyond his dream, but that century ran out and nobody did me that good office. During the second I made an oath that I would open all the treasures of the earth to any one that should set me at liberty, but with no better success. In the third I promised to make my deliverer a potent monarch, to be always near him in spirit, and to grant him every day three requests, of whatsoever nature they might be, but this century ran out, as well as the two former, and I continued in prison. At last, being angry at finding myself a prisoner so long, I swore that if afterwards any one should deliver me, I would kill him without mercy and grant him no other favor but to choose what kind of death he would die, and therefore, since you have delivered me to-day, I give you that choice."

This discourse afflicted the poor fisherman extremely. "I am very unfortunate," cried he, "to come hither to do such a piece of good service to one that is so ungrateful. I beg you to consider your injustice and revoke such an unreasonable oath. Pardon me and Heaven will pardon you; if you grant me my life, Heaven will protect you from all attempts against yours."

"No; your death is resolved upon," said the genie; "only choose how you will die."

Necessity is the mother of invention. The fisherman bethought himself of a stratagem. "Since I must die, then," he said to the genie, "I submit, but before I choose the manner of death I conjure you to answer me truly the question I am going to ask you."

The genie, finding himself obliged to give a positive answer, replied to the fisherman, "Ask what you will, but make haste."

When the genie had promised to speak the truth, the fisherman said to him, "I would know if you were actually in this vessel."

"Yes," replied the genie, "I was, and it is a certain truth."

"In good faith," answered the fisherman, "I cannot believe you; the vessel is not capable of holding one of your feet, and how is it possible that your whole body could lie in it?"

"Nevertheless I declare to you," replied the genie, "that I was there just as you see me here. Is it possible that you do not believe me?"

"Truly, not I," said the fisherman; "nor will I believe you, unless you show it me."

Upon this the body of the genie was dissolved and changed itself into smoke, extending itself as formerly upon the sea and along the shore; and then at last, being gathered together, it began to reënter the vessel, which it continued to do by a slow and equal motion in a smooth and exact way, till nothing was left out, and immediately a voice came forth, which said to the fisherman, "Well, now, incredulous fellow, I am all in the vessel; do you not believe me now?"

The fisherman, instead of answering the genie, took the cover of lead and speedily shut the vessel.

"Genie," cried he, "now it is your turn to beg my favor, and to choose which way I shall put you to death; but not so; it is better that I should throw you into the sea, from which I took you. Then I will build a house upon the bank, where I will dwell, to give notice to all fishermen who come to throw in their nets, to beware of such a wicked genie as you are."

The genie, enraged at these expressions, tried his utmost to get out of the vessel again, but finding it impossible, and perceiving that the fisherman had the advantage of him, he thought fit to dissemble his anger. " Fisherman," said he in a pleasant tone, " take heed you do not what you say, for what I spoke to you before was only by way of jest."

"O genie," replied the fisherman, "your crafty discourse will signify nothing to you, but to the sea you shall return. If you have stayed there already so long as you told me, you may very well stay there some time longer. I begged of you not to take my life, and you did reject my prayers; I am obliged to treat you in the same manner."

" My good friend fisherman," cried the genie, " I conjure you once more not to be guilty of such cruelty. Consider that it is not good to avenge one's self, and that, on the other hand, it is commendable to do good for evil."

" No," said the fisherman; " it is in vain to talk of letting you out; I am just going to throw you to the bottom of the sea."

"Hear me one word more," cried the genie; "I promise to do you no hurt; nay, far from that, I will show you a way to become exceedingly rich."

The hope of delivering his family from poverty prevailed with the fisherman. "I could listen to you," said he, "were there any credit to be given to your word."

The genie promised him faithfully, and at length the fisherman took off the covering of the vessel. At that very instant the smoke came out, and the genie, having resumed his form as before, kicked the vessel into the sea.

This action frightened the fisherman. "Genie," said he, "what is the meaning of that? Will you break the promise you have just made?"

The genie laughed at the fisherman's fear, and answered, "No, fisherman, be not afraid, I only did it to divert myself. To persuade you that I am in earnest, I bid you take your nets and follow me."

When they came to the side of a pond, the genie said to the fisherman, "Cast in your nets and catch fish."

The fisherman did not doubt he would catch some, because he saw a great number in the pond, but he was extremely surprised when he found they were of four colors—white, red, blue, and yellow. He threw in his nets and brought out one of each color. Never having seen the like, he could not but admire them, and judging that he might get a considerable sum for them, he was joyful.

"Carry those fish," said the genie, "and present them to your sultan. He will give you more money for them than ever you had in your life. You may come every day to fish in this pond, but I give you warning not to throw in your nets more than once a day; otherwise you will repent it. If you follow my advice, you will prosper."

Having spoken thus, he struck his foot upon the ground, which opened and swallowed him up and then closed again.

The fisherman, being resolved to follow the genie's advice exactly, forebore casting in his nets a second time. Very well satisfied with his catch, he returned to the town, making a thousand reflections upon his adventure.

He went straight to the sultan's palace to present his fish. The sultan was surprised when he saw the four fishes. He took them up one after another and, after having admired them a long time, said to his first vizier, "Take those fishes to the handsome cookmaid that the emperor of the Greeks sent me. I feel sure they must be as good to eat as they are to look at."

The vizier carried them himself to the cook, and delivered them into her hands. "Look you," said he; "there are four fishes newly brought to the sultan. He orders you to prepare them."

Then he returned to his master, who ordered him to give the fisherman four hundred pieces of gold.

The fisherman, who had never seen so much gold in his life, could scarcely believe his own good fortune, but thought it must be a dream. When he found it to be real, he at once provided necessities for his family with it.

Now, having told you what happened to the fisherman, I must acquaint you with what befell the sultan's cookmaid, whom we shall find in great perplexity.

She put the fish over the fire in a frying pan with oil, and when she thought them fried enough on one side, she turned them upon the other; but, O monstrous prodigy! scarce were they turned when the walls of the kitchen opened, and in came a young lady of wonderful beauty and comely size. She was clad in flowered satin, after the Egyptian manner, with pendants in her ears, and she wore bracelets of gold garnished with rubies and carried a rod of myrtle in her hand.

She came toward the frying pan — to the great amazement of the cookmaid, who stood immovable at the sight — and, touching one of the fishes with the end of the rod, said, "Fish, fish, art thou in thy duty?"

EGYPT

As the fish answered nothing, she repeated these words, and then the four fishes lifted up their heads all together and said to her, "Yes, yes; if you reckon, we reckon; if you pay your debts, we pay ours; if you fly, we overcome and are content."

As soon as they had uttered these words, the lady overturned the frying pan and entered into the wall, which shut and became as it was before.

The cookmaid was mightily frightened at this, and, coming to herself a little, went to take up the fishes that had fallen upon the hearth, but found them blacker than coal and not fit to be carried to the sultan. She fell to weeping most bitterly. "Alas!" said she, "what will become of me? If I tell the sultan what I have seen, he will not believe me, but will be enraged against me."

While she was thus bewailing, in came the grand vizier and asked her if the fishes were ready. She told him all that had happened, which we may easily imagine astonished him, but without speaking a word concerning it to the sultan he invented an excuse that satisfied him. He then sent for the fisherman and bade him bring four more such fish, saying a misfortune had befallen the others and they were not fit to be carried to the sultan. The fisherman told the vizier it was some trouble to get them, but he would certainly bring them the next day.

Accordingly the fisherman went away by night and, coming to the pond, threw in his nets betimes next morning, took four such fishes as the former, and brought them to the vizier at the hour appointed. The minister took them himself and shut himself up alone with the cookmaid. She put them over the fire, as she had done the four others the day before. When they were fried on one side and she had turned them on the other, the kitchen wall opened, and the same lady came in with the rod in her hand, touched one of the fishes and spoke to it as before, and all four gave her the same answer. After the four fishes had answered the young lady, she overturned the frying pan with her rod and retired into the same place in the wall from which she had come.

"This is too surprising and extraordinary," said the grand vizier, "to be concealed from the sultan. I will inform him of this prodigy." This he accordingly did.

The sultan was impatient to see the marvel himself. He sent for the fisherman and said to him, "Friend, cannot you bring me four more such fishes?"

The fisherman replied, "If your Majesty will be pleased to allow me three days' time, I will do it."

Having obtained his time, he went to the pond the next morning, and at the first throwing in of his net he caught four such fishes; he brought them presently to the sultan, who was all the more rejoiced at it, because he did not expect them so soon, and who gave him another four hundred pieces of gold.

As soon as the sultan had the fish, he ordered them to be carried into the closet, with all that was necessary for frying them. He shut himself up there with the vizier, who put them in the pan over the fire and when they were fried on one side turned them on the other. Then the wall of the closet opened, but instead of the young lady there came out a black man, in the habit of a slave and of a gigantic stature, with a great green staff in his hand.

He advanced toward the pan and, touching one of the fishes with his staff, said to it in a terrible voice, " Fish, art thou in thy duty? "

At these words the fishes raised up their heads and answered, " Yes, yes, we are; if you reckon, we reckon; if you pay your debts, we pay ours; if you fly, we overcome and are content."

The fishes had no sooner uttered these words than the black man threw the pan into the middle of the closet and reduced the fishes to a coal. He then retired fiercely and entered into the hole in the wall; it shut and appeared just as it did before.

The sultan, who was a brave man, resolved to go in person and inquire what it all meant. Therefore he got the direction to the place from the fisherman, dressed himself in a walking suit, and, with a scimitar in his hand, sallied forth alone upon the adventure.

I cannot tell you all his wonderful escapes from the power of the magician, but will merely say that he succeeded in discovering a palace, from which he released a very amiable young prince, who had been confined there a long time. He found that the fishes were formerly the servants belonging to this prince, and that they had been changed into fishes for endeavoring to release their master. They now regained their proper form; the palace of the magician was destroyed; the prince married the sultan's beautiful daughter; and the fisherman, who had been the cause of these happy events, was made a nobleman. Thus you see the genie was as good as his word in making the fisherman's fortune.

Adapted from The Arabian Nights

genie (jē′nĭ): a nature spirit, believed to be able to interfere in human affairs and to be sometimes subject to magic control. — **Mussulman** (mŭs′ŭl man): a Mohammedan (mō hăm′ĕd an), or follower of the prophet Mohammed (mō hăm′ĕd). — **Asaph** (ā′săf). — **genii** (jē′nĭ ī): the plural of *genie.*—**vizier**(vĭ zēr′): a high executive officer in Mohammedan countries; a minister or councilor of state. — **scimitar** (sĭm′ĭ tēr): a sword with a much-curved blade, used especially by Arabs and Persians.

MERCY

William Shakespeare

The quality of mercy is not strained,
It droppeth as the gentle rain from heaven
Upon the place beneath: it is twice blest;
It blesseth him that gives and him that takes:
'T is mightiest in the mightiest: it becomes
The thronèd monarch better than his crown;
His sceptre shows the force of temporal power,
The attribute to awe and majesty,
Wherein doth sit the dread and fear of kings;
But mercy is above this sceptred sway;
It is enthronèd in the hearts of kings,
It is an attribute to God himself;
And earthly power doth then show likest God's
When mercy seasons justice. Therefore, Jew,
Though justice be thy plea, consider this,
That, in the course of justice, none of us
Should see salvation: we do pray for mercy;
And that same prayer doth teach us all to render
The deeds of mercy.

From " The Merchant of Venice "

strained: restrained. — **Jew**: addressed to the merchant Shylock. This is a part of the speech in which Portia, disguised as a lawyer, pleads the cause of Antonio, the friend of her husband, against Shylock.

THE SUN IN EGYPT

GEORGE WILLIAM CURTIS

The sun is the secret of the East. There seems to be no light elsewhere. Italy simply preludes the Orient. Egyptian days are perfect. You breathe the sunlight; you feel it warm in your lungs and heart. The whole system absorbs sunshine, and all your views of life become warm and rich.

The Egyptian sun does not glare; it shines. The light has a creamy quality, soft and mellow, as distinguished from the intense whiteness of our American light. The forms of our landscape stand sharp and severe in the atmosphere, like frostwork, but the Eastern outlines are smoothed and softened. The sun is the mediator and blends beautifully the separate beauties of the landscape.

The sun shines in the brilliance of the colors the Easterns love. The sculptures upon the old tombs and temples are of the most positive colors,— red, blue, yellow, green, and black; and still the instinct is the same in the Egyptian costume, for golden and gay are the turbans wreathed around their dusky brows, and the buildings in which they sit (these wearers of the crimson and golden turbans, with their red slippers crossed under them), the walls of baths

EGYPT

A MOSQUE IN CAIRO

and cafés and mosques, are painted in the same gorgeous taste, with broad bars of red and blue and white. Over all this brilliance streams the intense sunshine, and completes what itself suggested. So warm, so glowing and rich, is the universal light and atmosphere that anything less than this in architecture would be unnatural. Strange and imperfect as it is, you feel the heart of nature throbbing all through Eastern art. Art there follows the plainest hints of nature, in the costume and architecture of to-day as in the antique architecture. The fault of oriental art springs from the very excess which is the universal law of Eastern life. It is the apparent attempt to say more than is sayable.

The child's faith, that the East lies near the rising sun, is absurd until you are there. Then you feel that the East was the first-born of the sun and inherits the larger share of his love and influence. Wherever your eye falls it sees the sun and the sun's suggestion. Egypt lies hard against his heart.

Adapted from " Nile Notes of a Howadji "

Italy simply preludes the Orient: The sunshine of Italy merely serves as an introduction to the sunshine of the East. — **mosque** (mŏsk): a Mohammedan place of worship.

AN ORIENTAL BAZAAR

George William Curtis

Eastern life is delightful in detail. It is a mosaic to be closely studied.

You enter the bazaar and the murmurous silence blends pleasantly with the luminous dimness of the place. The matting overhead, torn and hanging in strips, — along which, gilding them in passing, the sun slides into the interior, — is a heavy tapestry. The scene is a perpetual fair, such as is frequently met in Arabian stories.

Bedouins glide spectrally along, with wild, roving eyes, like startled deer. Sheiks from distant Asia, pompous effendi from Constantinople, Bagdad traders, sharp-eyed Armenian merchants, meet and mingle. All strange forms jostle and crowd in passing, and children, more beautiful than any others in the East, play in the living mazes of the crowd.

Shopping goes actively on. The merchant, without uncrossing his legs, exhibits his silks and coarse cottons to the long draped and veiled figures that group picturesquely about his niche. Your eye seizes the bright effect of all the gay goods as you saunter on. Here a merchant lays by his chibouk, and drinks

AN ARABIAN SHEIK

from a carved glass sweet liquorish water, cooled with snow from Lebanon. Here one closes his niche and shuffles off to the mosque, followed by his boy slave with the chibouk. Here another rises and bows

EGYPT

and falls, kissing the floor and muttering the noon prayer. Everywhere there is intense but languid life.

The bazaars are separated into kinds. That of the jewelers is inclosed, and you see the workers busily employed. Precious stones, miserably set, and handfuls of pearls, opals, and turquoises are quietly

AN ARABIAN VILLAGE ON THE BANKS OF THE NILE

presented to your inspection. There is no eagerness of traffic. A boy tranquilly hands you a ring, and another, when you have looked at the first. You say *la*, " no," and he retires. Or you pause over a clumsy silver ring, with an Arabic inscription upon the flint set in it. Golden Sleeve ascertains that it is the cipher of Hafiz. You reflect that it is silver, which is the orthodox metal, the Prophet having forbidden

A MOORISH SHOP

gold. You place it upon your finger with the stone upon the inside, for so the Prophet wore his upon the forefinger, that he might avoid ostentation. It is a quaint, characteristic, oriental signet ring. Hafiz is

EGYPT

a common name; it is probably that of the jeweler who owns the ring; but you have other associations with the name, and as you remember the Persian poet you suffer it to remain upon your finger, and pay the jeweler a few piasters. You do not dream that it is enchanted. You do not know that you have bought Aladdin's lamp, and, as a rub of that evoked omnipotent spirits, so a glance at your ring, when Damascus has become a dream, will restore you again to the dim bazaar, and to the soft eyes of the children that watch you curiously as you hesitate, and to the sweet inspiration of Syria.

Abridged from " The Howadji in Syria "

bazaar (bạ zär'): in the East a market place, more or less covered and lined with shops or stalls. — **sheik** (shēk): an Arab chief. — **effendi** (ĕ fĕn'dĭ): sir; a Turkish title of respect, applied especially to a state official or a man of learning. — **draped and veiled figures**: women; Turkish women always go abroad veiled. — **chibouk** (chĭ bōōk'): a Turkish pipe with a stem four or five feet long. — **la** (lä). — **Golden Sleeve**: the name of the author's guide. — **Hafiz** (hä'fĭz): the name of a celebrated Persian poet. — **the Prophet**: Mohammed. — **piasters** (pĭ ăs'tĕrz): small coins worth a fraction of a cent.

THE COMING OF THE PERSIAN EMBASSY

Georg Moritz Ebers

Cambyses, King of Persia, wished to marry Nitetis, the daughter of the Egyptian king, and sent his brother Bartia with a rich embassy into Egypt to escort the princess back to Persia.

An immense crowd was gathered at the harbor at Sais. Egyptians of every age and rank stood densely packed on the edge of the river. Soldiers and merchants in white robes trimmed with gaudy fringe, whose length indicated the rank of the wearer, mingled themselves with the herd of muscular, half-clothed men — the common people. Little children squeezed and pushed for the best places; women held up their babies that they might not lose the coveted sight. Constables with long staves, whose metal tops bore the name of the king, maintained order and quiet, taking especial care that no one was pushed into the waters of the Nile.

On the broad steps lined with sphinxes, which led down to the water from the garden of the palace, was an assemblage of a very different sort. Here, upon stone benches, sat the most honored of the priests, in long white garments, with gilded fillets on their heads and white staves in their hands. In their midst one could distinguish the chief judge by the waving ostrich feather in his cap (though some of the priests wore smaller ones) and by a costly amulet of sapphires which hung on a golden chain upon his breast. The captains of the Egyptian army wore parti-colored coats and in their belts short

AVENUE OF SPHINXES AT KARNAK

swords; a division of the bodyguard was stationed on the right of the steps; on the left were Greek soldiers in the Ionic dress.

In front of these, on a silver chair, sat the heir apparent to the throne, Psamtic, dressed in a close-fitting coat embroidered in gold. He was surrounded by the most eminent of the courtiers, chamberlains, councilors, and friends of the king, who carried flabella and wands tipped with golden lotus flowers in their hands.

The crowd vented their impatience by shouting and singing, while the priests and nobles sat in dignified silence on the steps opposite, each in his calmness looking like the great images which sat motionless in their places, gazing solemnly and fixedly on the eternal river.

Suddenly a lateen sail of scarlet and blue silk was seen in the distance. The people shouted with joy, " There they are! " " Take care, now! " " Nurse, hold the girl higher that she may see something! " " Look out now, Sebak, you'll push me into the water! " The officers, however, bringing into play their long rods, soon restored quiet.

The huge motley sails, easily distinguished among the hundred blue, white, and brown ones of the smaller Nile boats, came nearer and nearer to the expectant crowd. Then the heir apparent and the grandees rose from their places. The trumpeters of the king sounded a shrill fanfare of welcome as the first of the ships reached the steps. The vessel was richly gilded and bore on its beak the silver image of a sparrow hawk; in the midst of it stood a golden canopy with a scarlet top; under this lay large cushions; in the fore part of the ship, along the bulwarks, sat twelve rowers, their garments fastened

EGYPT

by costly braces. Under the canopy were six men gorgeously dressed and noble to look upon.

Before the ship had fairly touched the shore, the first to spring upon the steps was the youngest of them all, a glorious, fair-haired youth. At sight of

BOATS ON THE NILE

him, from the lips of many a young Egyptian an "Oh" of admiration escaped, and even the solemn expression of some of the dignitaries brightened into a pleasant smile. The cause of all this sensation, Bartia, the brother of the reigning king of Persia, had received from nature all that heart could ask.

From under the blue and white cloth which was woven round his tiara, thick golden hair escaped in wanton profusion; his blue eyes shone with life and mirth, kindness and mischief; pride, too, had a place there. His noble face was worthy to be the subject for a Grecian chisel, and his slender, muscular figure showed great strength and activity. His beauty was only equaled by the splendor of his dress. In the middle of the tiara which he wore gleamed a star of diamonds and turquoise. His upper garment of heavy white gold brocade, reaching to his knees, was fastened at the waist by a girdle of blue and white, the royal colors of Persia. He wore a short golden sword, whose handle and sheath were studded with white opals and blue turquoises; his pantaloons, gathered in at the ankles, half covered his bright blue leather shoes. His naked, sinewy arms, which the flowing sleeves of his dress allowed to be seen, were adorned with several costly bracelets of gold and precious stones, and from his slender neck a gold chain hung down upon his broad chest.

Following him came Darius, an illustrious young Persian of royal blood, dressed like Bartia but more plainly. The third was an old man with snow-white hair and a mild, pleasant face. He wore a long purple garment and was no other than Crœsus, the

EGYPT

dethroned king of Lydia, who was now living as a friend and adviser at the court of Cambyses. After him came the special ambassador of the king and two other Persian nobles.

Psamtic descended the steps to welcome the strangers; the dignitaries who followed him, letting their arms hang down, bowed almost to the ground before the newcomers. The Persians, their arms crossed upon their breasts, prostrated themselves before the Egyptian prince. When the first formalities were over, Bartia, after the custom of his country, kissed the cheek of the Egyptian prince, much to the astonishment of the people not accustomed to such a sight, and then betook himself with his hosts to the litters which were waiting to take him and his suite to the apartments assigned him in the palace.

Part of the crowd followed the foreigners, but most of the people stayed to see the spectacle of the disembarking of the rest of the ships.

Abridged from "An Egyptian Princess"

Ebers (ā'bĕrs). — **Nitetis** (nī tē'tĭs). — **Bartia** (bär'shạ). — **Sais** (sā'ĭs): an important city of ancient Egypt, in the Nile delta. — **fillets**: bands twisted about the hair. — **amulet** (ăm'ụ lĕt): an ornament or gem worn to protect one against evils. — **Ionic** (ī ŏn'ĭc): belonging to the district of Ionia. — **Psamtic** (săm'tĭc). — **flabella** (flạ bĕl'lạ): fans. — **lotus flowers**: Egyptian water lilies. — **lateen** (lạ tēn') **sail**: a triangular sail used in small boats in the Mediterranean and its tributaries. — **Sebak** (sĕb'ăk). — **Darius** (dạ rī'ụs). — **Crœsus** (krē'sụs): a very wealthy monarch who made war on Persia.

THE STATUES OF MEMNON.[1]

Walter Scott Perry

The modern city of Thebes is on the western bank of the Nile. Away to the north of it are the statues of Memnon, two colossal figures that have attracted the attention of nations almost from the dawn of history, and that tower far above fields of moving grain and guard the beautiful valley. Side by side they sit — silent, inscrutable, as if weighted with the responsibility of some secret whispered to them in the far-distant past. Each figure rises sixty-five feet above the ground, and each, with its pedestal, is estimated to weigh over one thousand tons. The legs from foot to knee measure twenty feet, while the middle finger of each hand is four and one half feet in length. When the Nile is at its highest level, the water rises above the pedestals of these seated figures.

The colossi of Memnon are all that remain of a temple erected by an ancient king. Just back of them rose a great pylon, or portal, leading to the court of the temple. Many traditions have come down to us regarding the musical sounds that formerly came from the northern statue, and that might

[1] Copyright, 1898, by The Prang Educational Company. Used by special permission.

be heard soon after sunrise. After the restoration of this statue by the Roman emperor Septimius Severus the musical sounds ceased. They were probably caused by the action of the sun's rays on the

THE STATUES OF MEMNON

moisture collected within the stones during the dews and damps of night. The cracks in the stones were plastered up, and ever after the statue was dumb.

From "Egypt, the Land of the Temple Builders"

Memnon (měm'nŏn): a name given by the Greeks to a colossal statue of King Amenophis III (ăm ĕ nō'fĭs), ruler of Egypt about 1410 B.C.— **colossi** (kŏ lŏs'ī): statues much larger than life. — **Septimius Severus** (sĕp tĭm'ĭ ŭs sĕ vē'rŭs): Roman emperor from 193 to 211 A.D.

THE HOUSE OF RHODOPIS

Georg Moritz Ebers

The Nile had overflowed its banks and spread itself far and wide over what were, but a little while before, rich grain fields and blooming gardens — an endless stretch of water as far as the eye could reach. The cities, guarded by their levees, with their gigantic temples and palaces, and the village roofs crowned with tall palms and acacias, were alone reflected in the river below. The boughs of the sycamore and plantain dipped into the stream, while the silvery poplars seemed to be trying to lift their upward-springing branches high above its reach. The full moon was pouring its soft light from beyond the Libyan hills, that faded far away into the western horizon; to the north, scarcely to be seen, lay the Mediterranean; on the water's surface floated the blue and the white lotus flowers; and through the night air, heavy with the scent of jasmine and acacia, flew bats of many kinds. In the tree tops slept the wild doves; pelicans, storks, and cranes crouched among the rushes on the river bank; the pelicans, sleeping with their great beaks under their wings, did not stir, but the cranes, startled by the stroke of the oars or the boatman's song, put out their long, thin necks, half in fear, half in curiosity. Not a breeze stirred, and the image of the moon, floating like a silver shield upon the water, showed that the Nile, which had taken the cataracts in a wild leap and had dashed past the giant temples of Upper

COLONNADE OF THE TEMPLE OF EDFU, UPPER EGYPT

Egypt in headlong flight, here, where it reached out to the sea with its hundred arms, had foregone its furious speed and given itself over to more gentle movement.

Upon this moonlight night, in the year 528 B.C., a boat passed up the almost unfelt current of the Canopean mouth of the Nile. An Egyptian sat on the high roof of the stern deck, and managed thence the long steering pole; in another part of the boat were the rowers, singing at their oars, while two men lay upon cushions placed on the deck under a canopy. Even by the light of the moon one could see that their faces were Hellenic. The elder, a large and muscular man of some sixty years, looked gloomily down into the stream, while his companion, younger by twenty years, now gazed up into the sky, now hailed the steersman, now gathered his beautiful purple chlamys into new folds. The boat had started two hours before from Naucratis, the only town in Egypt then open to the Greeks.

As the boat neared the shore the younger passenger arose and said to his fellow traveler: "We shall soon be at our goal, Aristomachus. Yonder, to the left, the house in the garden of palms that rises over the inundated flats, is the house of my friend Rhodopis. Her husband, Charaxus, who is now dead, built it for her, and all her friends, even the king himself, vie with each other in adorning it, year by year, with new beauties. Quite needless labor; the fairest ornament of the house, had they poured into it the treasures of the universe, will ever be its own noble mistress."

The old man raised himself, gave a passing look at the building, and said curtly, "What a paragon you make of this Rhodopis!"

EGYPT

Phanes smiled and answered in a self-satisfied tone, " I think I know something of men and women, and let me assure you that I know nothing in all Egypt grander than this gray-haired widow."

The boat at this moment reached the river wall of the garden, and with a light spring the Athenian, Phanes, leaped from the boat, while his companion followed him with a slow, steady step. The garden of Rhodopis, with its flowers, its perfumes, and its myriads of insects, seemed like a part of the land of fairies. Acanthus, yellow mimosas, hedges of snowball bushes, jasmines and lilacs, roses and laburnums, crowded each other; huge palms, acacias, and balsam trees towered over the bushes; great bats with delicate wings flitted through the air; and on the water were the distant sounds of song and laughter. An Egyptian had laid out this garden, and the builders of the Pyramids were from all time the most renowned landscape gardeners of the world; they understood the art of placing the flower beds, of arranging by rule the groups of trees and bushes, of giving to the canals, fountains, and arbors their places, of making for the walks their artistically fashioned hedges, and of dotting here and there ponds for gold and silver fish.

The house of Rhodopis was in the Grecian style. The exterior of the long one-story building would, according to our views, have been thought very simple; within, it united Egyptian color with Hellenic symmetry. The wide principal door opened upon the entrance hall of the house, on whose left side a large dining hall looked upon the river, while opposite to this was the kitchen, a room found only among the rich Greeks, the poorer people cooking their food at the hearth in the antechamber. The room for receiving visitors was at the farther opening of the entrance hall and in the form of a square surrounded by a gallery, into which several rooms opened. In the midst of this apartment there burned, upon an altar-shaped brazier of rich Ægina metal, the great fire of the house. During the day this room was lighted by means of openings in the roof, through which, at the same time, the smoke from the fire made its escape. Opposite to the entrance hall ran a passage terminated by a heavy door leading to the women's apartment, ornamented with pillars on three sides only; in this the women were accustomed to stay, except when sitting at their spinning and weaving in the rooms near the door opening into the yard. Between these and the rooms which extended along the women's apartment to the right and left, and which were used as guest chambers, lay the sleeping rooms, which were also used to hold the treasures of the house.

EGYPT

The walls of the reception hall were painted a reddish brown, against which the marble statues, gifts of an artist of Chios, stood out in strong relief. Heavy carpets from Sardis covered the floor. In front of the pillars lay cushions covered with tiger skins, while round the carved brazier were curiously shaped Egyptian chairs and finely cut tables of thya wood, upon which lay all sorts of musical instruments — flutes, lyres, etc. On the wall hung countless lamps—one representing a dolphin belching fire, another a strange winged creature whose jaws cast forth flames — all mingling their light with the blaze on the hearth.

In this hall stood several men of different appearance and various costumes. A Syrian from Tyre, in a rose-colored cloak, was having an animated conversation with a man whose sharply cut features and curly black hair showed the Israelite. The latter had come from his home to Egypt to buy for Zerubbabel, ruler of Judah, Egyptian horses and wagons, at that time greatly in repute. Near these stood three Greeks from Asia Minor, in the costly flowing garments of Miletus, talking earnestly with the simply clad ambassador of Delphi, who had come to collect moneys for the temple of Apollo. Rhodopis herself was talking with two Greeks from Samos; they spoke of art and poetry. The eyes of the Greek woman glowed with the fire of youth, her tall figure was straight and full her gray hair curled in waves round her well-shaped head, and was twisted at the back into a net of delicate gold thread. Her fair forehead was crowned with a sparkling diamond. The noble Hellenic face was pale but beautiful, and without a wrinkle, in spite of her advanced age. Every one supposed Rhodopis to be much younger than she really was, though she never assumed the youth which she did not possess. All her movements were those of matronly dignity, and her grace was not that of youth, which tries to please, but that of age, which shows forth its graciousness, demanding and receiving respect.

At this moment our two travelers appeared in the hall. The eyes of all turned toward them, and when Phanes entered, leading his friend by the hand, he was welcomed most heartily.

One of the Milesians exclaimed, " I have been trying all this while to find out what was missing. Now it is perfectly clear that without Phanes there is no mirth! "

Another cried in a deep voice, " Mirth is a good thing, and if you bring it with you, you are welcome, Athenian! "

" To me," said Rhodopis, going to meet her new guests, " you are most welcome if you are happy, and no less welcome if oppressed with trouble, for I have

EGYPT

no greater joy than to smooth the lines of care from the forehead of a friend. You too, O Spartan," she said, turning to Aristomachus, "I call a friend, for every one is that who is dear to those I care for."

Adapted from "An Egyptian Princess"

Rhodopis (rŏ dō'pĭs). — **Edfu** (ĕd'foo): a town in Upper Egypt; its temple is the most perfect existing example of an ancient Egpytian religious edifice. — **Canopean** (kăn ŏ pē'an) **mouth**: the Nile has several mouths, near one of which the ancient city of Canopus (ka nō'pus) stood. — **Hellenic** (hĕ lĕn'ĭk): Greek, from *Hellas* (hĕl'as), the ancient name for Greece. — **chlamys** (klă'mĭs): a Greek cloak. — **Naucratis** (nau'kra tĭs). — **Aristomachus** (ăr ĭs tŏm'a kus). — **Charaxus** (ka răx'us). — **Phanes** (fā'nĕz). — **Athenian** (a thē'nĭ an): a citizen of Athens, the chief city of central Greece. — **Ægina** (ē jī'na) **metal**: Ægina was a large island near Athens containing mines of copper and silver. — **Chios** (kī'ŏs): an island in the Ægean (ē jē'an) Sea. — **Sardis** (sär'dĭs): the ancient capital of Lydia, a flourishing city under Crœsus. — **thya** (thī'a) **wood**: the sweet-smelling wood of an African tree. — **Tyre** (tīr). — **Zerubbabel** (zĕ rŭb'a bĕl): a leader of the Jews at the time of the Babylonian captivity; he was appointed governor of Judea (joo dē'a) by the Babylonian king, and led the first band of the Jewish exiles who returned to Palestine. — **Miletus** (mī lē'tus): a Greek city in Asia Minor. — **Delphi** (dĕl'fī): a town in central Greece famous for the temple and oracle of Apollo. — **Samos** (sā'mŏs): one of the principal islands in the Ægean Sea. — **Spartan**: a citizen of Sparta (spär'ta), the chief city of southern Greece.

ANTONY AND CLEOPATRA

After the death of Julius Cæsar, the great Roman general and emperor, there was civil war in the Roman commonwealth. Augustus Cæsar and Mark Antony were the chiefs of one party and Brutus and Cassius of the other. Brutus and Cassius were killed in a battle at Philippi and their army was broken up. Augustus Cæsar then went back to Italy, but Antony went on to Asia. In Asia there were still some of the party of Brutus and Cassius, and the king of Parthia was promising to help them. There was danger, also, that Cleopatra, the queen of Egypt, might be on that side.

While he was making preparation for the Parthian war, Antony sent his lieutenant, Dellius, to command Cleopatra to make her appearance in Cilicia, to answer an accusation that in the late wars she had given assistance to Cassius. Dellius had no sooner seen her face and remarked her adroitness and subtlety in speech, than he bade her go to Cilicia in her best attire and to fear nothing from Antony, the gentlest and kindest of soldiers. He well knew that Antony would not molest a woman like this.

Cleopatra had some faith in the words of Dellius, but more in her own attractions. She made great preparation for her journey, of money, gifts, and ornaments of value, such as so wealthy a kingdom might afford, but her surest hopes were in her own magic arts and charms.

EGYPT

She received several letters to summon her, but she took no account of these orders, and at last, as if in mockery of them, she came sailing up the river Cydnus in a barge with gilded stern and outspread sails of purple, while oars of silver beat time to the

ANTONY AND CLEOPATRA
After the painting by Alma-Tadema

music of flutes and fifes and harps. She herself lay under a canopy of cloth of gold, dressed as Venus in a picture, and beautiful young boys, like painted cupids, stood on each side to fan her. Her maids were dressed like sea nymphs and graces, some steering at the rudder, some working at the ropes.

The perfumes diffused themselves from the vessel to the shore, which was covered with multitudes, part following the galley up the river on either bank, part running out of the city to see the sight. The market place was quite emptied, and Antony at last was left alone, sitting upon the tribunal, while the word went through all the multitude that Venus was come for the common good of Asia.

On her arrival Antony sent to invite her to supper. She thought it more fitting that he should come to her; so, willing to show his good humor and courtesy, he complied and went. He found the preparations to receive him magnificent beyond expression, but nothing so admirable as the great number of lights, for on a sudden there was let down all together so great a number of branches, with lights in them so ingeniously disposed, some in squares and some in circles, that the whole thing was a spectacle that has seldom been equaled for beauty.

The next day Antony invited her to supper and was very desirous to outdo her in magnificence as well as in contrivance, but he found he was altogether beaten in both, and was so well convinced of it that he was himself the first to jest and mock at his poverty of wit and his rustic awkwardness.

Her actual beauty, it was said, was not so remarkable, but her presence was irresistible. It was a

EGYPT

pleasure merely to hear the sound of her voice, with which, like an instrument of many strings, she could pass from one language to another, so that there were few of the barbarian nations that she answered by an interpreter. To most of them she spoke herself, — to the Ethiopians, Hebrews, Arabians, Syrians, Medes, Parthians, and many others, whose language she had learned; this was all the more surprising because most of the kings, her predecessors, scarcely gave themselves the trouble to acquire the Egyptian tongue.

Antony was so captivated by her that he suffered himself to be carried away to Alexandria, there to keep holiday, like a boy, in play and diversion, squandering and fooling away in enjoyments that most costly of all valuables — time.

Adapted from Plutarch's " Parallel Lives "

Antony (ăn'tŏ nĭ): Cæsar's friend. — **Cleopatra** (klē ŏ pā'tra). — **Julius Cæsar** (jōōl'yus sē'zar). — **Augustus** (au gŭs'tus): Julius Cæsar's nephew and successor. — **Brutus** (brōō'tus) **and Cassius** (kăsh'ĭ us): two of the conspirators against Cæsar. — **Philippi** (fĭ lĭp'ī): a town in Greece. — **Parthia** (pär'thĭ a): an ancient country in the southwestern part of Asia. — **Dellius** (děl'ĭ us). — **Cilicia** (sĭ lĭsh'ĭ a): an ancient Roman province in southwestern Asia. — **Cydnus** (sĭd'nus). — **Alma-Tadema** (ăl'ma-tăd'ĕ ma). — **Venus** (vē'nus): goddess of love. — **cupid** (kū'pĭd): the little god of love, son of Venus. — **contrivance**: clever arrangement. — **Ethiopians** (ē thĭ ō'pĭ anz): inhabitants of Ethiopia, in ancient geography considered to be part of the upper Nile valley. — **Medes** (mēdz). — **Plutarch** (plōō'tärk): a celebrated Greek writer living in the first century. — **"Parallel Lives"**: a book containing the biographies of forty-six Greeks and Romans.

CLEOPATRA

William Shakespeare

Enobarbus

The barge she sat in, like a burnished throne,
Burned on the water: the poop was beaten gold;
Purple the sails, and so perfumèd that
The winds were love-sick with them; the oars were
    silver,
Which to the tune of flutes kept stroke, and made
The water which they beat to follow faster,
As amorous of their strokes. For her own person,
It beggared all description: she did lie
In her pavilion — cloth-of-gold of tissue —
O'er-picturing that Venus where we see
The fancy outwork nature: on each side her
Stood pretty dimpled boys, like smiling Cupids,
With divers-coloured fans whose wind did seem
To glow the delicate cheeks which they did cool,
And what they undid did.

Agrippa
                O, rare for Antony!

Enobarbus

Her gentlewomen, like the Nereides,
So many mermaids, tended her i' the eyes,

EGYPT

And made their bends adornings: at the helm
A seeming mermaid steers: the silken tackle
Swell with the touches of those flower-soft hands,
That yarely frame the office. From the barge
A strange invisible perfume hits the sense
Of the adjacent wharfs. The city cast
Her people out upon her; and Antony,
Enthronèd i' the market-place, did sit alone,
Whistling to the air; which, but for vacancy,
Had gone to gaze on Cleopatra too
And made a gap in nature.

              AGRIPPA
                    Rare Egyptian!

From "Antony and Cleopatra"

Enobarbus (ĕn ŏ bär′bŭs). — barge: pleasure boat. — amorous (ăm′ŏ-rŭs) of: loving. — beggared: made poor. — cloth-of-gold of tissue: gold embroidery on a ground of tissue. — O'er-picturing: picturing again. — what they undid did: the colored fans, even while they made a cooling breeze, cast a glow which made the queen's face appear flushed. — Agrippa (ȧ grĭp′ȧ). — Nereides (nē rē′ĭ dēz): sea nymphs. — tended her i' the eyes: "waited upon her in her sight and made their service an added adornment." — yarely frame: cleverly perform. — adjacent wharfs: crowds upon the wharfs. — enthronèd: Antony was sitting in state in the market place, awaiting her. — but for vacancy: except that it would have made a vacuum in nature — a thing impossible. — Had gone: would have gone.

THE KNOWLEDGE OF THE ANCIENT EGYPTIANS

Recent researches have proved that many of the inventions which we call modern were well known to the ancient Egyptians. They built railroads; they tipped buildings with lightning rods; in building their pyramids and temples they handled great masses of stone that no modern engineer would know how to handle; they made glass of rainbow hues; they built arches with precision unsurpassed at the present day; they painted frescoes in colors that have lasted; they built pyramids and temples that have defied time.

They excelled in all the arts. They made paper so excellent in quality that it exists to-day. The art of making fine linen and other fabrics was well known to them. Joseph was presented by Pharaoh with a vesture of fine linen, a gold chain, and other beautiful things. The linen was dyed in brilliant and gorgeous colors, the secret of which is now among the lost arts. On ancient Egyptian mummies we often find the most beautiful embroidery and bead work. Their jewelry of gold, silver, and precious stones was wonderfully wrought.

The Egyptians were proficient in all mathematical sciences. They measured land; they divided time and

EGYPT

PILLARS AT KARNAK

knew the true length of the year. They recorded the rising and setting of the stars, and they engraved these observations on their monuments, a record dating back many thousands of years. The entrance to the Great Pyramid points to the North Star, and there is no doubt that even when that famous tomb was built, there were those who understood the precession of the equinoxes and the zodiac.

A great unknown past, tens of centuries at least, must lie behind the Egypt that created Memphis and the pyramids. A famous archæologist has recently said: "Egypt is far from being exhausted. Its soil contains enough to occupy twenty centuries of workers, for what has come to light is comparatively nothing."

There are mysteries and mysteries concerning ancient Egypt that may yet be unveiled. The answer to many a problem of life lies back of the inscrutable smile of the stony sphinx.

precession of the equinoxes (ē′kwĭ nŏx ĕz): a difficult subject for those ignorant of modern science. It has to do with the change in direction of the earth's axis, which causes a slow, backward movement of the points at which the sun is said to "cross the equator."—**zodiac** (zō′dĭ ăk): a broad imaginary belt in the heavens, including the paths of the moon and the principal planets, and having the sun's path in the center. The zodiac has twelve divisions, or signs, formerly marked by constellations bearing the same names. Owing to the precession of the equinoxes the signs and the constellations no longer correspond. — **archæologist** (är kē ŏl′ŏ jĭst): one who has studied the art, architecture, customs, and beliefs of ancient peoples, as shown in their monuments, inscriptions, etc.

THE NUMBER OF THE STARS

Sir Robert Stawell Ball

To count the stars involves a task which lies beyond the power of man. Even without the aid of a telescope we can see a great multitude of stars from any part of the earth. One great astronomer, with the patience to count them, estimated that there are about six thousand visible to the naked eye.

But if you look through even a small telescope, you will be astonished at the enormous multitude of stars that are disclosed.

Take, for instance, the constellation in the north called the Great Bear, or the Great Dipper, circling about the North Star. The dipper is made of four large stars forming a sort of oblong, with three more stars that represent the handle. Now, on a fine clear night, count how many stars you can see within the oblong of the dipper. They are all very faint, but you will be able to see a few; with good sight you may count perhaps ten. Next, take an opera glass and look in the same place. If you carefully count the stars you can now see within the dipper, you will find fully two hundred. So the opera glass shows you twenty times as many stars as you can see without its aid. A small telescope will show you one hundred times as many as your eyes could reveal. Even now we are only at the beginning of the count; the very great telescopes add largely to the number.

The Milky Way, the telescope tells us, is made up of multitudes and multitudes of stars, so small and faint that we cannot distinguish them individually; we see only the white glow produced by the millions and millions of stars shining in the broad band.

Adapted from " Star-Land "

THE WONDERS OF THE HEAVENS

Praise ye the Lord: for it is good to sing praises unto our God.

He telleth the number of the stars; he calleth them all by their names.

Great is our Lord, and of great power: his understanding is infinite.

Psalm cxlvii

Then the Lord answered Job out of the whirlwind, and said,

Where wast thou when I laid the foundations of the earth? declare, if thou hast understanding.

Who hath laid the measures thereof, if thou knowest? or who hath stretched the line upon it?

Whereupon are the foundations thereof fastened? or who laid the corner stone thereof;

When the morning stars sang together, and all the sons of God shouted for joy?

Hast thou commanded the morning since thy days; and caused the dayspring to know his place?

Canst thou bind the sweet influences of Pleiades, or loose the bands of Orion?

Job xxxviii

Pleiades (plē′yạ dēz): a crowded cluster of stars in the constellation Taurus. — **Orion** (ō rī′ọn): one of the brightest constellations.

THE CHILD AND THE WIND

Lucy Lyttleton

Child

What wind is this across the roofs so softly makes
  his way,
That hardly makes the wires to sing, or soaring
  smoke to sway?

Wind

I am a weary southern wind that blows the live-
  long day
  Over the stones of Babylon, of Babylon,
The ruined walls of Babylon, all fallen in decay.

Oh, I have blown o'er Babylon when royal was
  her state,
When fifty men in gold and steel kept watch at
  every gate,
When merchantmen and boys and maids thronged
  early by and late
  Under the gates of Babylon, of Babylon,
The marble gates of Babylon, when Babylon was
  great.

Child

Good weary wind, a little while pray let your course
  be stayed,

EGYPT

And tell me of the talk they held, and what the people said,
The funny folk of Babylon before that they were dead,
    That walked abroad in Babylon, in Babylon,
Before the towers of Babylon along the ground were laid.

Wind

The folk that walked in Babylon, they talked of wind and rain,
Of ladies' looks, of learnèd books, of merchants' loss and gain,
How such-a-one loved such-a-maid that loved him not again,
    (For maids were fair in Babylon, in Babylon;)
Also the poor in Babylon of hunger did complain.

Child

But this is what the people say as on their way they go,
Under my window in the street; I heard them down below.

Wind

What other should men talk about, five thousand years ago?
    For men they were in Babylon, in Babylon,
That now are dust in Babylon I scatter to and fro.

THE MOURNING ATHENA

GREECE

NAUSICAA[1]

Translated by William Cullen Bryant

    After the siege of Troy, Ulysses, one of the Greek chieftains, set out for his home in Ithaca. He bore many hardships, but Pallas Athene, the goddess of wisdom, aided him. She has just saved him from shipwreck and guided him to the shores of Phæacia, the realm of King Alcinoüs. Ulysses, exhausted from his buffetings, is sleeping in a grove near the "place of the lavers."

Now to his [Alcinoüs'] palace, planning the return
Of the magnanimous Ulysses, came
The blue-eyed goddess Pallas, entering
The gorgeous chamber where a damsel slept, —
Nausicaa, daughter of the large-souled king
Alcinoüs, beautiful in form and face
As one of the immortals. . .
The shining doors were shut. But Pallas came
As comes a breath of air, and stood beside
The damsel's head and spake. In look she seemed

[1] Used by permission of, and by special arrangement with, Houghton Mifflin Company, authorized publishers of Bryant's translation of the Odyssey.

The daughter of the famous mariner
Dymas, a maiden whom Nausicaa loved,
The playmate of her girlhood. In her shape
The blue-eyed goddess stood, and thus she said: —
  " Nausicaa, has thy mother then brought forth
A careless housewife? Thy magnificent robes
Lie still neglected, though thy marriage day
Is near, when thou art to array thyself
In seemly garments, and bestow the like
On those who lead thee to the bridal rite;
For thus the praise of men is won, and thus
Thy father and thy gracious mother both
Will be rejoiced. Now with the early dawn
Let us all hasten to the washing-place.
I too would go with thee, and help thee there,
That thou mayst sooner end the task, for thou
Not long wilt be unwedded. . . .
                    Make thy suit at morn
To thy illustrious father, that he bid
His mules and car be harnessed to convey
Thy girdles, robes, and mantles marvellous
In beauty. That were seemlier than to walk,
Since distant from the town the lavers lie."
  Thus having said, the blue-eyed Pallas went
Back to Olympus, where the gods have made,
So saith tradition, their eternal seat.
The tempest shakes it not, nor is it drenched

GREECE

By showers, and there the snow doth never fall....
And in the golden light, that lies on all,
Day after day the blessèd gods rejoice.
Thither the blue-eyed goddess, having given
Her message to the sleeping maid, withdrew.

    Soon the bright morning came. Nausicaa rose,
Clad royally, as marvelling at her dream
She hastened through the palace to declare
Her purpose to her father and the queen.
She found them both within. Her mother sat
Beside the hearth with her attendant maids,
And turned the distaff loaded with a fleece
Dyed in sea-purple. On the threshold stood
Her father, going forth to meet the chiefs
Of the Phæacians in a council where
Their noblest asked his presence. Then the maid,
Approaching her belovèd father, spake: —

    " I pray, dear father, give command to make
A chariot ready for me, with high sides
And sturdy wheels, to bear to the river-brink,
There to be cleansed, the costly robes that now
Lie soiled. Thee likewise it doth well beseem
At councils to appear in vestments fresh
And stainless. Thou hast also in these halls
Five sons, two wedded, three in boyhood's bloom,
And ever in the dance they need attire
New from the wash. All this must I provide."

She ended, for she shrank from saying aught
Of her own hopeful marriage. He perceived
Her thought and said: " Mules I deny thee not,
My daughter, nor aught else. Go then; my grooms
Shall make a carriage ready with high sides
And sturdy wheels, and a broad rack above."

    He spake, and gave command. The grooms obeyed,
And, making ready in the outer court
The strong-wheeled chariot, led the harnessed mules
Under the yoke and made them fast; and then
Appeared the maiden, bringing from her bower
The shining garments. In the polished car
She piled them, while with many pleasant meats
And flavoring morsels for the day's repast
Her mother filled a hamper, and poured wine
Into a goatskin. . . .

                       Nausicaa took
The scourge and showy reins, and struck the mules
To urge them onward. Onward with loud noise
They went, and with a speed that slackened not,
And bore the robes and her, — yet not alone,
For with her went the maidens of her train.
Now when they reached the river's pleasant brink,
Where lavers had been hollowed out to last
Perpetually, and freely through them flowed
Pure water that might cleanse the foulest stains,

GREECE

They loosed the mules, and drove them from the wain
To browse the sweet grass by the eddying stream;
And took the garments out, and flung them down
In the dark water, and with hasty feet
Trampled them there in frolic rivalry.
And when the task was done, and all the stains
Were cleansed away, they spread the garments out
Along the beach and where the stream had washed
The gravel cleanest. . . .
And now, when they were all refreshed by food,
Mistress and maidens laid their veils aside
And played at ball. Nausicaa the white-armed
Began a song. . . .

   Now when they were about to move for home
With harnessed mules and with the shining robes
Carefully folded, then the blue-eyed maid,
Pallas, bethought herself of this, — to rouse
Ulysses and to bring him to behold
The bright-eyed maiden, that she might direct
The stranger's way to the Phæacian town.
The royal damsel at a handmaid cast
The ball; it missed, and fell into the stream
Where a deep eddy whirled. All shrieked aloud.
The great Ulysses started from his sleep
And sat upright, discoursing to himself; —

   "Ah me! upon what region am I thrown?
What men are here, — wild, savage, and unjust,

Or hospitable, and who hold the gods
In reverence? There are voices in the air,
Womanly voices, as of nymphs that haunt
The mountain summits, and the river-founts,
And the moist grassy meadows." . . .
  Thus having said, the great Ulysses left
The thicket. . . .
          To right and left they fled
Along the jutting river-banks. Alone
The daughter of Alcinoüs kept her place,
For Pallas gave her courage and forbade
Her limbs to tremble. So she waited there.
             . . . With gentle words
Skilfully ordered thus Ulysses spake: —
  " O queen, I am thy suppliant, whether thou
Be mortal or a goddess. If perchance
Thou art of that immortal race who dwell
In the broad heaven, thou art, I deem, most like
To Dian, daughter of imperial Jove,
In shape, in stature, and in noble air.
If mortal and a dweller of the earth,
Thrice happy are thy father and his queen,
Thrice happy are thy brothers; and their hearts
Must overflow with gladness for thy sake,
Beholding such a scion of their house
Enter the choral dance. But happiest he
Beyond them all, who, bringing princely gifts,

GREECE

Shall bear thee to his home a bride; for sure
I never looked on one of mortal race,
Woman or man, like thee, and as I gaze
I wonder. . . .
         Now upon this shore some god
Casts me, perchance to meet new sufferings here;
For yet the end is not, and many things

GODS FROM THE PARTHENON FRIEZE

The gods must first accomplish. But do thou,
O queen, have pity on me, since to thee
I come the first of all. I do not know
A single dweller of the land beside.
Show me, I pray, thy city." . . .

And then the white-armed maid Nausicaa said: —
... "The city I will show thee, and will name
Its dwellers, — the Phæacians, — they possess
The city; all the region lying round
Is theirs, and I am daughter of the prince
Alcinoüs, large of soul, to whom are given
The rule of the Phæacians and their power."
So spake the damsel, and commanded thus
Her fair-haired maids: "Stay! whither do ye flee,
My handmaids, when a man appears in sight?
Ye think, perhaps, he is some enemy.
Nay, there is no man living now, nor yet
Will live, to enter, bringing war, the land
Of the Phæacians. Very dear are they
To the great gods. We dwell apart, afar
Within the unmeasured deep, amid its waves
The most remote of men; no other race
Hath commerce with us. This man comes to us
A wanderer and unhappy, and to him
Our cares are due. The stranger and the poor
Are sent by Jove, and slight regards to them
Are grateful. Maidens, give the stranger food
And drink." . . .
She spake; they heard and cheerfully obeyed,
And set before Ulysses food and wine.
The patient chief Ulysses ate and drank
Full eagerly, for he had fasted long.

GREECE

    White-armed Nausicaa then had other cares.
She placed the smoothly folded robes within
The sumptuous chariot, yoked the firm-hoofed mules,
And mounted to her place, and from the seat
Spake kindly, counselling Ulysses thus: —
    " Now, stranger, rise and follow to the town,
And to my royal father's palace I
Will be thy guide, where, doubt not, thou wilt meet
The noblest men of our Phæacian race.
        . . . I will lead thee in the way. . . .
Go quickly through the palace till thou find
My mother where she sits beside the hearth, . . .
And clasp my mother's knees; so mayst thou see
Soon and with joy the day of thy return,
Although thy home be far." . . .
                      Ulysses toward
The gorgeous palace of Alcinoüs turned
His steps, yet stopped and pondered ere he crossed
The threshold. For on every side beneath
The lofty roof of that magnanimous king
A glory shone as of the sun or moon.
There from the threshold, on each side, were walls
Of brass that led towards the inner rooms,
With blue steel cornices. The doors within
The massive building were of gold, and posts
Of silver on the brazen threshold stood,

And silver was the lintel, and above
Its architrave was gold; and on each side
Stood gold and silver mastiffs, the rare work
Of Vulcan's practised skill, placed there to guard
The house of great Alcinoüs, and endowed
With deathless life, that knows no touch of age.
Along the walls within, on either side,
And from the threshold to the inner rooms,
Were firmly planted thrones on which were laid
Delicate mantles, woven by the hands
Of women. The Phæacian princes here
Were seated. . . .
                        Fifty maids
Waited within the halls, where some in querns
Ground small the yellow grain; some wove the web
Or twirled the spindle, sitting, with a quick
Light motion, like the aspen's glancing leaves.
The well-wrought tissues glistened as with oil.
As far as the Phæacian race excel
In guiding their swift galleys o'er the deep,
So far the women in their woven work
Surpass all others. Pallas gives them skill
In handiwork and beautiful design.
Without the palace-court, and near the gate,
A spacious garden of four acres lay.
A hedge enclosed it round, and lofty trees
Flourished in generous growth within, — the pear

GREECE

And the pomegranate, and the apple-tree
With its fair fruitage, and the luscious fig
And olive always green. . . .
   Ulysses, the great sufferer, standing there,
Admired the sight; and when he had beheld

CARYATID PORCH IN ERECHTHEUM

The whole in silent wonderment, he crossed
The threshold quickly, . .
        . . . hastened through the hall and came
Close to Arete and Alcinoüs,
The royal pair. Then did Ulysses clasp
Arete's knees. . . .
             Thus Ulysses prayed: —
 "Arete, daughter of the godlike chief

Rhexenor! to thy husband I am come
And to thy knees, from many hardships borne,
And to these guests, to whom may the good gods
Grant to live happily, and to hand down,
Each one to his own children, in his home,
The wealth and honors which the people's love
Bestowed upon him. Grant me, I entreat,
An escort, that I may behold again
And soon my own dear country. I have passed
Long years in sorrow, far from all I love."

   He ended, and sat down upon the hearth
Among the ashes, near the fire, and all
Were silent utterly. At length outspake
Echeneus, oldest and most eloquent chief
Of the Phæacians; large his knowledge was
Of things long past. With generous intent,
And speaking to the assembly, he began:—

   "Alcinoüs, this is not a seemly sight,—
A stranger sitting on the hearth among
The cinders. All the others here await
Thy order, and move not. I pray thee, raise
The stranger up, and seat him on a throne
Studded with silver." . . .

   This when the reverend king Alcinoüs heard,
Forthwith he took Ulysses by the hand,—
That man of wise devices,— raised him up
And seated him upon a shining throne,

GREECE

From which he bade Laodamas arise,
His manly son, whose seat was next to his. . . .
Alcinoüs took the word, and thus he said: —
 "Princes and chiefs of the Phæacians, hear.
I speak as my heart bids me. Since the feast
Is over, take your rest within your homes.
To-morrow shall the Senators be called
In larger concourse. We will pay our guest
Due honor in the palace, worshipping
The gods with solemn sacrifice. And then
Will we bethink us how to send him home,
That with no hindrance and no hardship borne
Under our escort he may come again
Gladly and quickly to his native land." . . .
 When Morn appeared, the rosy-fingered child
Of Dawn, Alcinoüs, mighty and revered,
Rose from his bed. Ulysses, noble chief,
Spoiler of cities, also left his couch. . . .
Nausicaa, goddess-like in beauty, stood
Beside a pillar of that noble roof,
And looking on Ulysses as he passed,
Admired, and said to him in wingèd words: —
 "Stranger, farewell, and in thy native land
Remember thou hast owed thy life to me."
 Ulysses, the sagacious, answering said: —
"Nausicaa, daughter of the large-souled king
Alcinoüs! so may Jove, the Thunderer,

Husband of Juno, grant that I behold
My home, returning safe, as I will make
To thee as to a goddess day by day
My prayer; for, lady, thou hast saved my life."

Abridged from the Odyssey of Homer

Nausicaa (nau sĭk'å ạ). — **Ulysses** (û lĭs'ēz). — **Ithaca** (ĭth'ạ kạ): an island off the western coast of Greece. — **Pallas Athene** (păl'as ạ thē'nê): the Greek name for Minerva (mĭ nẽr'va). — **Phæacia** (fē ā'shạ): a land sometimes identified with Corcyra (kŏr sĭ'rạ), an island near Ithaca. — **Alcinoüs** (ăl sĭn'ô ụs). — **lavers** (lā'vẽrz): basins for washing. — **Dymas** (dī'mas). — **sea-purple**: Tyrian purple, or royal purple, a dye made from a shellfish and so costly that only kings could use it. — **Dian** (dī'ăn): Diana (dī ăn'ạ), the goddess of the moon. — **Jove** (jōv): the king of the gods. *Jove* and *Jupiter* are Latin names for this god; *Zeus* (zūs) is the Greek name. — **Parthenon** (pär'thē nŏn): a temple on the Acropolis (ạ krŏp'ô lĭs) at Athens. — **lintel**: a horizontal piece of timber over a door or window. — **architrave** (är'kĭ trāv): a beam, or a beamlike layer of stone or other material, crossing the tops of a row of columns and supporting a roof or a wall above. — **Vulcan** (vŭl'kạn): the blacksmith of the gods; he was skilled in all fine metal work. — **quern** (kwẽrn): a hand mill for grinding grain. — **Arete** (ä rē'tē). — **caryatid** (kăr ĭ ăt'ĭd): a statue of a woman; it was used in buildings as a support in place of a column. — **Erechtheum** (ĕr ĕk thē'ụm): a temple on the Acropolis. — **Rhexenor** (rĕks ē'nŏr). — **Echeneus** (ĕk ẹ nē'ụs). — **Laodamas** (lå ŏd'ạ mạs). — **Juno** (jōō'nō). — **Odyssey** (ŏd'ĭ sĭ): Homer's poem telling about the wanderings of Ulysses, whose name in Greek was Odysseus (ô dĭs'ūs).

THE RETURN OF ULYSSES

Charles Lamb

When the great city of Troy was taken, the Greek chieftains set sail for their homes; but there was wrath in heaven against them, for they had borne themselves haughtily in the day of their victory. Therefore they did not all find a safe and happy return; many were shipwrecked, and of them all the wise Ulysses was he who wandered farthest and suffered most. He escaped the enchantments of Circe, the dangers of Scylla and Charybdis, came back to his course whence the winds of Æolus had driven him far, and at last was allowed to come to his own land.

Here the goddess Athena met him and told him that his wife Penelope was almost a prisoner in her own home. The nobles of Ithaca and of the neighboring lands, believing Ulysses to be dead, were urging Penelope to marry some one of them. They were living in his house as owners rather than as guests, lording and domineering at their pleasure; but Penelope, who had always believed that Ulysses would return, had refused her many suitors.

So Athena changed Ulysses in appearance into a very old man clad in tattered rags, and gave him a staff to support his steps. Then she sent him to his herdsman Eumæus, strictly charging him that he should reveal himself to no man except to his own son Telemachus. Eumæus received the old beggar kindly, bewailing much that his good master Ulysses did not return and that he was forced to work so long for evil men who hated him.

A READING FROM HOMER
After the painting by Alma-Tadema

And the old beggar answered him, " My friend, I say to you solemnly, Ulysses shall return. Within this year, nay, ere this month be fully ended, your eyes shall behold Ulysses in his own palace, righting the wrongs of his wife and his son. "

Then came to supper the servants of the herdsman, who had been out all day in the fields. After supper the beggar, who had eaten well and was refreshed, told the eager herdsmen tales that related to their king Ulysses and to the wars of Troy.

When morning was come, Ulysses made offer to depart; but as he spoke the steps of one crossing the court were heard, and a noise of dogs fawning and leaping about as if for joy. Eumæus said: " It is the step of Telemachus, the son of King Ulysses. He has heard that there is here one who brings tidings of his father."

Ulysses covered his eyes with his hands, that the prince might not see the tears that stood in them. And Telemachus said, " Is this the man who can tell us tidings of the king my father?"

Then, as Eumæus had departed to see to some necessary business, Athena suddenly stood at the door. She gave signs to Ulysses that the time was now come when he should make himself known to his son, and by her great power she changed him back into his own shape.

But Telemachus, who saw now a king in the vigor of his age, where but just before he had seen an old beggar, was struck with fear, and, thinking it was some god, he turned away his eyes. But his father cried: "Look better at me; I am no god. I am but thy father; I am that Ulysses whose absence has exposed thy youth to so many wrongs." Then he kissed his son, nor could he any longer keep back the tears.

Then said Ulysses again: "I am he that after twenty years' absence has seen at last my own country. It was Athena that changed me as you saw."

And Ulysses gave directions to his son to return to the house, but to impart this secret to no one, not even to the queen his mother. And he charged him to hold himself ready, for he should follow shortly in his beggar's likeness, and together they would drive out the wicked suitors. And Telemachus departed, promising to obey, and Ulysses became again a beggar in base and beggarly attire.

So Ulysses came to his own palace and crept by turns to each of the suitors as they sat at meat, holding out his hand for alms. And some pitied him and gave him alms, but the greater part reviled him and bade him begone as one that spoiled their feast.

Now Telemachus sat at meat with the suitors and knew that it was the king his father who begged an alms. And when his father came to him, he gave him of his own meat, and of his own cup to drink. And the suitors were angry to see a pitiful beggar so honored by the prince, and they said, "Prince Telemachus does ill to encourage wandering beggars."

"I see," said Ulysses, "that a poor man should get but little at your board." And one of the suitors, angered by this speech, snatched up a stool and smote the beggar upon the neck and shoulders. But Ulysses said nothing more, for the time was not yet come.

Now Ulysses had not seen his wife Penelope, for the queen did not care to mingle with the suitors at their banquets, but, as became one that had been Ulysses' wife, kept much in private, spinning and weaving among her maids. But Ulysses now went to her, and the maids said, " It is the beggar who came to court to-day." Then Penelope said, " It may be that he has traveled and has heard something concerning Ulysses."

So the beggar stood before the queen, and she knew him not to be Ulysses, but supposed that he was some poor traveler. And she asked him questions, but he did not tell her as yet who he was.

Now there was a bow that Ulysses had left when he went to Troy. It had been out of use and unstrung since that time, for no other man had strength to draw that bow. And Athena put it into the mind of Telemachus to propose to the suitors to try who was strongest. And he promised that to the man who should be able to draw the bow his mother should be given in marriage.

So Telemachus set up a mark and the bow was brought into the midst. The chief among the suitors had the first offer. He took the bow and, fitting an arrow to the string, strove to bend it, but not with all his might and main could he draw the ends of the bow together. Then they softened the string with fat, and one by one they tried, but not one could stir the string.

Then Ulysses prayed that he might try, and immediately a clamor was raised among the suitors, who scorned that a beggar should seek to contend in a game of such noble mastery. But Telemachus ordered that the bow should be given to him, since they had all failed.

Then Ulysses took the bow into his hand and surveyed it in all parts, to see if it had become stiff. He found it in good condition and with ease drew the string of his own tough bow, and as he let it go it twanged with such a shrill noise as a swallow makes when it sings through the air. Then he fitted an arrow to the bow, and, drawing it to the head, he sent it right to the mark which the prince had set up.

Whereupon the rags fell from his shoulders, and his own kingly likeness returned. Telemachus advanced to his side, also armed. Then Ulysses revealed himself to all and said that he was the man whom they held to be dead at Troy, whose palace they had usurped and whose wife they had annoyed. And he dealt his deadly arrows among them, and there was

GREECE

no avoiding them. And Athena in the likeness of a bird sat upon the beam which went across the hall, and clapped her great wings with a fearful noise.

Then certain of the queen's household went up and told Penelope what had happened, and how her lord Ulysses was come home and had driven out the suitors, and they said, "That poor guest whom you talked with last night was Ulysses." But the queen thought they mocked her, and would not believe it.

By this time Telemachus and his father were come to where the queen was. And when she saw Ulysses, she stood motionless and had no power to speak. And Telemachus called to her that it was his father. Then she doubted no longer, but ran and fell upon Ulysses' neck. And to him his long labors and his severe sufferings seemed as nothing, now that he was restored to his home and his wife and son.

So from that time the land had rest from the suitors, and the happy Ithacans sang songs of praise to the gods for the safe return of their king.

Adapted from "The Adventures of Ulysses"

Circe (sir′sē): an enchantress who changed some of Ulysses' companions into swine. — **Scylla** (sĭl′a̤) **and Charybdis** (ka̤ rĭb′dĭs): monsters who devoured seamen; supposed to personify a projecting rock and a whirlpool in the Straits of Messina (mĕ sē′na̤), between Italy and Sicily; hence the saying, "Escape Scylla to fall into Charybdis." — **Æolus** (ē′ō lṳs): the god of the winds. — **Penelope** (pĕ nĕl′ō pē). — **Eumæus** (ū mē′ṳs). — **Telemachus** (tĕ lĕm′a̤ kṳs). — **Alma-Tadema** (ăl′ma̤ tăd′ĕ ma̤).

[113]

HOW JASON WENT TO SCHOOL

Charles Kingsley

This is the tale of a boy who became a hero. Now if a boy is to become a hero when he is a man, he must have good training first. So this is the tale of Jason's training, which he had from the strangest schoolmaster ever heard of. Jason was the little lad who, when he was grown, called together a band of heroes called Argonauts and, as their leader, sailed away with them to a distant land to win the Golden Fleece.

Whither they sailed no one knows exactly. It all happened so long ago that it has grown dim, like a dream of last year. Why they went, or what the Golden Fleece was, we cannot tell; some say that the Fleece was just yellow gold. Perhaps it was, but we know there is a better thing on earth than wealth, a better thing than life itself, and that is, to have done something, before you die, for which good men may honor you and God your Father smile upon you.

Therefore we will believe — why should we not? — that the Argonauts were noble men who planned and did a noble deed, and that because of this their fame has lived and been told in story and song, mixed up, no doubt, with dreams and fables and yet true and right at heart. So we like to know how Jason got his training, for each of us has a Golden Fleece to seek, and a wild sea to sail over ere we reach it, and dragons to fight ere it be ours.

The father of this little lad was called Æson, and he was king of a kingdom by the sea, and ruled over many heroes. But he had a stepbrother named Pelias, who grew up fierce and lawless and did many a fearful deed. At last he drove out Æson and took the kingdom to himself, and he ruled over the heroes by the sea.

And Æson, when he was driven out, went sadly away out of the town, leading his little son by the hand. He said to himself, "I must hide the child in the mountains, or Pelias will surely kill him, because he is the heir."

So he went up from the sea, through the vineyards and the olive groves, toward Pelion, the ancient mountain whose brows are white with snow.

He went up and up into the mountain, till the boy was tired and footsore and Æson had to bear him in his arms. At last he came to the mouth of a lonely cave at the foot of a mighty cliff.

From the mouth of the cave came the sound of music and a man's voice singing to the harp.

Then Æson put down the lad and whispered, "Fear not, but go in, and whomsoever you shall find, lay your hand upon his knees and say, 'In the name of Zeus, the father of gods and men, I am your guest from this day forth.'"

Then the lad went in without trembling, for he too was a hero's son. But when he was within, he stopped in wonder, to listen to that magic song.

There he saw the singer lying upon bearskins and fragrant boughs. It was Chiron, the ancient centaur, the wisest of all beings beneath the sky. Down to the waist he was a man, but below he was a noble horse. His white hair rolled down over his broad shoulders, and his white beard over his broad brown chest, and his eyes were wise and mild, and his forehead was like a mountain wall.

And in his hand he held a harp of gold, and struck it with a golden key, and as he struck he sang till his eyes glittered and filled all the cave with light. And he sang of the birth of time, and of the heavens and the dancing stars, and of the ocean, and the fire, and the shaping of the wondrous earth. And he sang of the treasures of the hills, and the hidden jewels of the mine, and the veins of fire and metal, and the virtues of all healing herbs, and of the speech of birds, and of prophecy, and of hidden things to come.

Then he sang of health and strength and manhood and a valiant heart, and of music and hunting,

GREECE

and of wrestling and all the games which heroes love, and of travel and wars and sieges and a noble death in fight; and then he sang of peace and plenty, and of equal justice in the land. And as he sang the boy listened wide-eyed and forgot his errand in the song.

At last old Chiron was silent, and with a soft voice called the lad. And the lad ran trembling to him and would have laid his hand upon his knees, but Chiron smiled and said: "Call hither your father Æson, for I know you and all that has happened. I saw you both afar in the valley, even before you left the town."

Then Æson came in sadly, and Chiron asked him, "Why came you not yourself to me, Æson?"

And Æson said: "I thought, 'Chiron will pity the lad if he sees him come alone,' and I wished to try whether he was fearless and dare venture like a hero's son. But now I entreat you by Father Zeus, let the boy be your guest till better times, and train him among the sons of the heroes, that he may do his work in the land."

Then Chiron smiled and drew the lad to him, and laid his hand upon his golden locks and said, "Are you afraid of my horse's hoofs, fair boy, or will you be my pupil from this day?"

"I would gladly have horse's hoofs like you, if I could sing such songs as yours," answered the boy.

And Chiron laughed and said, "Sit here by me till sundown, when your playfellows will come home, and you shall learn like them to be a king worthy to rule over gallant men."

Then he turned to Æson and said: "Go back in peace and bend before the storm like a prudent man. This boy shall become a glory to you and to the house of your fathers."

And Æson wept over his son and went away, but the boy did not weep, so full was his fancy of that strange cave, and the centaur, and his song, and the playfellows whom he was to see.

Then Chiron put the lyre into his hands and taught him how to play it, till the sun sank low behind the cliff and a shout was heard outside.

And then in came the sons of the heroes, Æneas and Hercules and Theseus and many another mighty name. And great Chiron leaped up joyfully, and his hoofs made the cave resound as the boys shouted: "Come out, Father Chiron, come out and see our game. Come and hear what we have done."

And Chiron praised them all, each according to his deserts.

Then some of the lads brought in wood and split it and lighted a blazing fire; others prepared the meat and set it to roast before the fire. And while the meat was cooking they bathed in the snow torrent

GREECE

and washed away the dust and sweat. And then all ate till they could eat no more (for they had tasted nothing since the dawn) and drank of the clear spring water. And when the remnants were put away, they all lay down upon the skins and leaves

THE THESEUM

about the fire, and each took the lyre in turn and sang and played with all his heart.

And after a while they all went out to a plot of grass at the cave's mouth, and there they boxed and ran and wrestled and laughed till the stones fell from the cliffs. Then Chiron took his lyre, and all the lads joined hands, and as he played they danced to the music, in and out and round and round.

And the little lad danced with them, delighted, and then slept a wholesome sleep upon fragrant leaves of bay and myrtle and marjoram and flowers of thyme, and rose at the dawn and bathed in the torrent, and became a schoolfellow to the heroes' sons and forgot all his former life. But he grew strong and brave upon the pleasant fields of Pelion, in the keen mountain air. And he learned to wrestle

YOUNG HORSEMEN, FROM THE PARTHENON FRIEZE

and to box and to hunt and to play upon the harp; and next he learned to ride, for old Chiron used to mount him on his back; and he learned the virtues of all herbs and how to cure all wounds, and Chiron called him Jason the Healer, and that is his name until this day.

And ten years came and went, and Jason was grown to be a mighty man. Hercules was gone to Thebes, to fulfill those famous labors which have become a proverb among men. And Æneas was gone home to Troy, whence he sailed, as you will read, to discover Italy and lay the foundation for a great Roman empire.

So Chiron sent Jason forth, for he knew that his time had come. But first he asked him to promise two things: to speak harshly to no soul whom he met, and to stand by every word he should speak.

Jason wondered, but he promised, and then he leaped down the mountain, to take his fortune like a man.

Adapted from "The Argonauts"

Jason (jā'sǫn). — **Argonauts** (är'gǒ nauts): the fifty heroes who followed Jason; so called because they sailed in a ship called the *Argo*. — **Æson** (ē'sǫn). — **Pelias** (pē'lĭ ạs). — **Pelion** (pē'lĭ ǫn). — **Chiron** (kī'rŏn). — **centaur** (sĕn'taur). Notice the rhythmical swing of Kingsley's prose. — **Æneas** (ĕ nē'ạs): the founder of Rome. — **Hercules** (hĕr'cŭ lēz): a mighty Greek hero of great courage and physical strength. — **Theseus** (thē'sūs): one of the Argonauts and a great hero; he was a king of Athens. — **Theseum** (thĕ sē'ụm): a temple in Athens where it was supposed Theseus was buried.

THE SPARTANS' MARCH

Felicia Dorothea Hemans

'Twas morn upon the Grecian hills,
   Where peasants dressed the vines,
Sunlight was on Cithæron's rills,
   Arcadia's rocks and pines.

And brightly, through his reeds and flowers,
   Eurotas wandered by,
When a sound arose from Sparta's towers
   Of solemn harmony.

Was it the hunters' choral strain
   To the woodland goddess poured?
Did virgin hands in Pallas' fane
   Strike the full-sounding chord?

But helms were glancing on the stream,
   Spears ranged in close array,
And shields flung back a glorious beam
   To the morn of a fearful day!

And the mountain echoes of the land
   Swelled through the deep blue sky,
While to soft strains moved forth a band
   Of men that moved to die.

GREECE

They marched not with the trumpet's blast,
    Nor bade the horn peal out;
And the laurel groves, as on they passed,
    Rang with no battle-shout!

They asked no clarion's voice to fire
    Their souls with an impulse high;
But the Dorian reed and the Spartan lyre
    For the sons of liberty!

And still sweet flutes, their path around,
    Sent forth Æolian breath;
They needed not a sterner sound
    To marshal them for death!

So moved they calmly to their field,
    Thence never to return,
Save bearing back the Spartan shield,
    Or on it proudly borne!

Hemans (hĕm′anz). — **Cithæron** (sĭ thē′rŏn): a mountain in Greece. — **Arcadia** (är kā′dĭ a̯): a district of southern Greece. — **Eurotas** (ū rō′tas): a river of Greece. — **fane**: a temple or church. — **Dorian** (dō′rĭ an) **reed**: a musical instrument made of a hollow reed, used by the Dorians. — **Æolian** (ē ō′lĭ an): pertaining to the wind, from Æolus, god of the winds.

THE WINGÈD VICTORY OF SAMOTHRACE

A VICTOR OF THE GAMES

William Stearns Davis

The sacred games celebrated at Olympia, Delphi, Nemea, and Corinth exerted a tremendous influence upon the life of ancient Hellas. Myers, in his " Eastern Nations and Greece," says: " The competitors must be of the Hellenic race; must have undergone special training in the gymnasium; and must, moreover, be unblemished by any crime against the state or sin against the gods. Spectators from all parts of the world crowded to the festival. The victor was crowned with a garland of sacred olive; heralds proclaimed his name abroad; his native city received him as a conqueror, sometimes through a breach made in the city walls."

The story describes a scene at Eleusis. Glaucon, an Athenian, is returning, a victor, from the Isthmian games at Corinth. His wife, Hermione, and her father, Hermippus, are waiting to welcome him as he passes through Eleusis on his way to Athens.

A cluster of white stuccoed houses with a craggy hill behind, and before them a blue bay girt in by the rocky isle of Salamis — thât is Eleusis-by-the-Sea. Eastward and westward spreads the teeming Thriasian plain, richest in Attica. Behind the plain the encircling mountain wall fades away into a purple haze. One can look southward toward Salamis; then to the left rises the rounded slope of brown Pœcilon, sundering Eleusis from its greater neighbor, Athens. The stony hill slopes are painted red by countless poppies. One hears the tinkling of the bells of roving goats. At the very foot of the hill rises a temple with proud columns and pediments — the fane of Demeter, the Earth Mother, and the seat of her Mysteries, renowned through Hellas.

The house of Hermippus, first citizen of Eleusis, stood to the east of the temple. On three sides the gnarled trunks and somber leaves of the sacred olives almost hid the low white walls of the rambling buildings. On the fourth side, facing the sea, the dusty road wound west toward Megara. Here, by the gate, were gathered a rustic company: brown-faced village lads and lasses, toothless graybeards, cackling old wives. Above the barred gate swung a festoon of ivy, while from within the court came the squeaking of pipes, the tuning of citharas, and shouted orders — signs of a mighty bustling. Then, even while the company grew, a half-stripped courier flew up the road and into the gate.

"They come," ran the wiseacres' comment, but their buzzing ceased as again the gate swung back to suffer two ladies to peer forth. Ladies in truth, for the twain had little in common with the ogling village maids, and whispers were soon busy with them.

"Look — his wife and her mother! See, she lifts her pretty blue veil; I'm glad she's handsome."

The two ladies were clearly mother and daughter, of the same noble height and dressed alike in white.

GREEK COSTUMES
After the painting by J. Coomans

Both faces were framed in a flutter of Amorgos gauze: the mother's was saffron, crowned with a wreath of golden wheat ears; the daughter's, blue with a circlet of violets. And now, as they stood with arms entwined, the younger brushed aside her veil. The gossips were right. The robe and the crown hid all but the face and a tress of lustrous brown hair — but that face! Had not King Hephæstus wrought every line of clear Phœnician glass, then touched them with snow and rose, and shot through all the ichor of life? Hermione was indeed the worthy daughter of a noble house, and happy the man who was faring homeward to Eleusis!

Another messenger! Louder bustle in the court and the voice of Hermippus arraying his musicians! Now a sharp-faced man, who hid his bald pate under a crown of lilies, joined the ladies — Conon, father of the victor. Then a third runner, this time in his hand a triumphant palm branch, and his one word " Here! " A crash of music answered from the court, while Hermippus, a stately nobleman, his fine head just sprinkled with gray, led out his unmartial army.

Single pipes and double pipes, tinkling lyres and many-stringed citharas, not to forget herdsmen's reed flutes, cymbals, and tambours, all made melody and noise together. An imposing procession wound out into the Corinth road.

GREECE

Here was the demarch of Eleusis, a pompous worthy who could hardly hold his head erect, thanks to an exceedingly heavy myrtle wreath; after him, two by two, the snowy-robed, long-bearded priests of Demeter; behind these the noisy corps of musicians; and then a host of young men and women — bright of eye, graceful of movement — twirling long chains of ivy, laurel, and myrtle in time to the music. Palm branches were everywhere. The procession moved down the road, but even as it left the court a crash of cymbals through the olive groves answered its uproar. Deep now and sonorous sounded manly voices as in some triumphal chant. Hermione, as she stood by the gate, drew closer to her mother. Inflexible Attic custom seemed to hold her fast. No noblewoman might thrust herself boldly under the public eye, — save at a sacred festival, — no, not even when the center of the gladness was her husband.

"He comes!" So she cried to her mother; so cried every one. Around the turn in the olive groves swung a car in which Cimon stood proudly erect, and at his side another. Marching before the chariot were Themistocles, Democrates, Simonides; behind followed every Athenian who had visited the Isthmia. The necks of the four horses were wreathed with flowers; flowers hid the reins and bridles, the chariot, and even its wheels. The victor stood aloft, his scarlet cloak flung back, displaying his godlike form. An unhealed wound marred his forehead, — Lycon's handiwork, — but who thought of that, when above the scar pressed the wreath of wild parsley? As the two processions met, a cheer went up that shook the red rock of Eleusis. The champion answered with his frankest smile; only his eyes seemed questioning, seeking some one who was not there.

"Io! Glaucon!" The Eleusinian youths broke from their ranks and fell upon the chariot. The horses were loosed in a twinkling. Fifty arms dragged the car onward. The pipers swelled their cheeks, each trying to outblow his fellow. Then after them sped the maidens. They ringed the chariot round with a maze of flower chains. As the car moved they accompanied it with a dance of unspeakable ease, modesty, and grace. Youths and maidens burst forth into singing.

> "Io! Io, pæan! the parsley-wreathed victor hail!
> Io! Io, pæan! sing it out on each breeze, each gale!
>   He has triumphed, our own, our beloved,
>   Before all the myriad's ken.
>   He has met the swift, has proved swifter!
>   The strong, has proved stronger again!
>   Now glory to him, to his kinsfolk,
>   To Athens, and all Athens' men!
>   Meet, run to meet him,
>   The nimblest are not too fleet.

GREECE

> Greet him, with raptures greet him,
>   With songs and with twinkling feet.
> He approaches, — throw flowers before him,
>   Throw poppy and lily and rose;
> Blow faster, gay pipers, faster,
>   Till your mad music throbs and flows,
> For his glory and ours flies through Hellas,
>   Wherever the Sun-King goes.
> Io! Io, pæan! crown with laurel and myrtle and pine,
> Io, pæan! haste to crown him with olive, Athena's dark vine."

Matching action to the song, they threw over the victor crowns and chains beyond number, till the parsley wreath was hidden from sight. Near the gate of Hermippus the jubilant company halted. The demarch bawled long for silence, won it at last, and approached the chariot. He, good man, had been a long day meditating on his speech of formal congratulation, and enjoyed his opportunity. Glaucon's eyes still roved and questioned, yet the demarch rolled out his windy sentences. But then occurred something unexpected. Even as the magistrate took breath after reciting the victor's noble ancestry, there was a cry, a parting of the crowd, and Glaucon leaped from the chariot. The veil and the violet wreath fell from the head of Hermione. Then even the honest demarch cut short his eloquence to swell the salvo.

"The beautiful to the beautiful! The gods reward well. Here is the fairest crown!" For all

Eleusis loved Hermione and would have forgiven far greater things from her than this.

. . . .

Hermippus feasted the whole company, — the crowd at long tables in the court, the chosen guests in a more private chamber. "Nothing to excess" was the truly Hellenic maxim of the refined Eleusinian, and he obeyed it. His banquet was elegant without any gluttony. The Syracusan cook had prepared a lordly turbot; there was no vulgar gorging with meat, after the Bœotian manner. The aromatic honey was the choicest from Mount Hymettus.

Since the smaller company was well selected, convention was waived and ladies were present. Hermione sat on a wide chair beside her comely mother, her younger brothers on stools at either hand. Directly across the narrow table Glaucon and Democrates reclined on the same couch.

The dinner ended toward evening. The whole company escorted the victor on his way to Athens. At Daphni, the pass over the hills, the archons and strategi — highest officials of the state — met them with cavalry and torches and half the city trailing at their heels. Twenty cubits of the city walls were pulled down to make a gate for the triumphal entry. There was another great feast at the government house. The purse of a hundred drachmæ, due by

GREECE

law to Isthmian victors, was presented. A street was named for Glaucon in the new port town of Piræus. Simonides recited a triumphal ode. All Athens, in short, made merry for days.

Abridged from "A Victor of Salamis"

Samothrace (săm′ô thrās). — **Olympia** (ô lĭm′pĭ a). — **Nemea** (nĕ′mĕ a). — **Corinth** (kŏr′ĭnth): a city on the Isthmus, southwest of Athens. — **Eleusis** (ê lū′sĭs). — **Glaucon** (glau′kon). — **Hermione** (hĕr mī′ô nē). — **Hermippus** (hĕr mĭp′pus). — **Salamis** (săl′a mĭs). — **Thriasian** (thrĭ ā′shĭ an). — **Attica** (ăt′ĭ ka): a district of Greece of which Athens was the capital. — **Pœcilon** (pē′sĭ lŏn). — **pediment** (pĕd′ĭ mĕnt): a low, triangular part resembling a gable, crowning the fronts of Greek buildings, especially porticoes. — **Demeter** (dĕ mē′tĕr): Greek name for Ceres (sē′rēz), goddess of agriculture. — **Mysteries**: secret religious ceremonies. — **Megara** (mĕg′a ra): a city between Athens and Corinth. — **cithara** (sĭth′a ra): a musical instrument resembling the guitar. — **Amorgos** (ă môr′gŏs): an island in the Ægean Sea. — **Hephæstus** (hĕ fĕs′tus): the god of fire and workmanship; the Roman name was *Vulcan.* — **Phœnician** (fĕ nĭsh′an): from Phœnicia, north of Palestine. — **ichor** (ī′kŏr): a fluid supposed to supply the place of blood in the veins of the gods. — **Conon** (kō′non). — **demarch** (dē′märk): head of one of the wards into which Athens was divided. Eleusis and other small towns in Attica were counted as divisions of the great city. — **Cimon** (sī′mon): a great statesman and general. — **Themistocles** (thĕ mĭs′tô klēz): a famous Greek statesman and politician. — **Democrates** (dĕ mŏc′rá tēz). — **Simonides** (sī mŏn′ĭ dēz): a famous Greek poet. — **Isthmia** (ĭs′mĭ a): the Corinthian games. — **Lycon** (lī′kon). — **Io** (ī′ô): hail. — **pæan** (pē′an): praise. — **salvo** (săl′vô): burst of applause. — **Syracusan** (sĭr a kū′san): from *Syracuse*, a city in Sicily, renowned for its high living. — **turbot** (tûr′bot): a fish. — **Bœotian** (bē ō′ shan): pertaining to Bœotia, a province northwest of Athens. — **Hymettus** (hī mĕt′us). — **Daphni** (dăf′nī). — **archon** (är′kŏn); **strategi** (stra tē′jī): chief officers of the state. — **cubit** (kū′bĭt): a measure of length, about eighteen inches. — **drachma** (drăk′ma): a Greek coin worth about eighteen cents; plural, *drachmæ* (drăk′mē). — **Piræus** (pī rē′us): the seaport of Athens.

THE MIRACULOUS PITCHER

Nathaniel Hawthorne

One evening in the long ago, old Philemon and his old wife Baucis sat at their cottage door, enjoying the sunset. They had eaten their frugal supper and were talking about their garden and their cows and their beehives and their grapevines, which clambered over the cottage wall and on which the grapes were beginning to turn purple.

A great clamor rose from the village below them. "Ah, wife," said Philemon, "I fear some poor traveler is seeking rest, and our neighbors have set their dogs at him, as usual."

"Welladay," answered old Baucis, "I do wish they felt a little more kindness."

These old folks, you must know, were quite poor. Their food was seldom anything but bread, milk, vegetables, and now and then a bunch of grapes that had ripened against the cottage wall. But they were two of the kindest people in the world and would cheerfully have gone without their dinners any day, rather than refuse a slice of their brown loaf, or a cup of new milk, to a weary traveler.

"I never heard the dogs so loud!" observed the good old man.

"Nor the children so rude!" answered his good old wife; for it must be explained that the people in the village even encouraged their children to run after poor strangers, and to shout at their heels and pelt them with stones.

The noise came nearer and nearer, and finally two travelers approached, the dogs at their heels. Once or twice the younger of the two men, who was slender and active, turned about and drove back the dogs with his staff. His companion, who was very tall, walked calmly on, as if disdaining to notice either the naughty children or the pack of curs.

"Go you and meet them," said Baucis, "while I make haste within doors, and see whether we can get them anything for supper."

Philemon went, with hearty words of welcome on his lips, to help the strangers up the hill. But to his surprise the younger man seemed not at all wearied with a long day's journey. He was dressed in an odd way, with a sort of cap on his head, the brim of which stuck out over both ears. He had on a singular pair of shoes, too, and his feet seemed wonderfully light and active, as if he could hardly keep them on the ground.

"I used to be light-footed in my youth," said Philemon, "but I always found my feet grow heavier toward nightfall."

"There is nothing like a good staff to help one along," answered the stranger.

It was an odd-looking staff. It was made of olive wood and had something like a little pair of wings near the top. Two snakes, carved in the wood, were represented as twining themselves about the staff.

"Friends," said the old man, "sit down and rest on this bench. My good wife Baucis has gone to see what you can have for supper. We are poor folk, but you shall be welcome to whatever we have."

The younger stranger threw himself on the bench, letting his staff fall, but presently the staff seemed to get up from the ground of its own accord, and, spreading its little pair of wings, it half hopped, half flew, and leaned itself against the wall of the cottage.

Before Philemon could ask any questions, the elder stranger spoke to him. "Was there not," he asked, "a lake, in ancient times, where yonder village now stands?"

"Not in my day, friend," answered Philemon, "nor in my father's time."

"It was so once," said the stranger, in a deep, stern voice. "And since the people of yonder village have forgotten the affections and sympathies of their nature, it were better the lake were there again."

The traveler looked so stern that Philemon was almost frightened. It grew darker suddenly, and

MERCURY
From the statue by Giovanni da Bologna

there was a roll of thunder in the air, but a moment afterwards the stranger's face became so kindly and mild that Philemon forgot his terror.

The three talked sociably together while Baucis was getting supper.

"Pray, my young friend," said Philemon, after laughing at the witty remarks of the younger stranger, "what may I call your name?"

"If you call me Quicksilver," answered the traveler, "the name will fit tolerably well."

"Quicksilver?" repeated Philemon. "It's a very odd name! And your companion there, has he as strange a one?"

"You must ask the thunder to tell it you," replied Quicksilver mysteriously. "No other voice is loud enough."

Philemon gazed in awe at the elder stranger. Never did a grander figure sit more humbly beside a cottage door. When he talked, it was in such a way that Philemon wanted to tell him everything in his heart.

But Philemon, simple and kind-hearted old man, had not many secrets to disclose. He talked about his life. His wife Baucis and himself had dwelt in that cottage from their youth, earning their bread by honest labor, always poor but still contented. He told what excellent butter and cheese Baucis made, and how nice were the vegetables he raised in his garden.

He said, too, that because they loved one another so much it was the wish of both that they might die, as they had lived, together.

The stranger listened and smiled. "You are a good old man," said he, "and you have a good wife. It is fit that your wish be granted."

Baucis now came out and began to make apologies for the poor supper.

"Had we known you were coming," said she, "my good man and myself would have gone without our supper, but I took most of the milk to-day to make cheese, and our last loaf is already half eaten. Ah, me! I never feel the sorrow of being poor save when a poor traveler knocks at our door."

"All will be well," replied the elder stranger. "An honest welcome works miracles with the food."

"A welcome you shall have," cried Baucis, "and likewise a little honey and a bunch of purple grapes besides."

"Why, Mother Baucis, it is a feast!" exclaimed Quicksilver, laughing. "I think I never felt hungrier in my life."

"Mercy on us!" whispered Baucis to her husband. "If the young man has such a terrible appetite, there will not be half enough supper."

They all went into the cottage. And what should Quicksilver's staff do but spread its little wings and go hopping and fluttering up the doorsteps! Tap, tap, went the staff on the kitchen floor; nor did it rest until it had stood itself beside Quicksilver's chair.

As Baucis had said, it was a scanty supper. There was a piece of a brown loaf, a bit of cheese, and a dish of honey. There was a pretty good bunch of grapes for each of the guests. A moderately sized earthen pitcher, nearly full of milk, stood at a corner of the board, but when Baucis had filled two bowls, only a little milk remained in the bottom of the pitcher.

The travelers drank all the milk in their two bowls at a draft.

"A little more milk, kind Mother Baucis, if you please," said Quicksilver. "The day has been hot, and I am very much athirst."

"Now, my good people," answered Baucis, in great confusion, "I am so sorry and ashamed, but there is hardly a drop more milk in the pitcher. O husband! husband! why did n't we go without our supper?"

"Why," cried Quicksilver, taking the pitcher by the handle, "matters are not quite so bad."

So saying, to the vast astonishment of Baucis, he filled not only his bowl but his companion's, from the pitcher that was supposed to be almost empty.

"But I am old," thought Baucis, "and apt to be forgetful. I must have made a mistake."

"What excellent milk!" said Quicksilver. "My kind hostess, I must really ask you for a little more."

Now Baucis knew there could not possibly be any milk left, but, to show him how the case was, she lifted the pitcher and made a motion as if pouring milk into Quicksilver's bowl. What was her surprise when a cascade of milk fell bubbling into the bowl and filled it to the brim. And what a fragrance that milk had!

"Now a slice of your brown loaf, Mother Baucis," said Quicksilver, "and a little of that honey."

The loaf, when Baucis and her husband ate of it, had been rather dry; now it was light and moist. Baucis tasted of a crumb; it was more delicious than bread ever was before. And that honey! Its color was of gold; it had the odor of a thousand flowers, but of such flowers as never grew in an earthly garden!

Baucis found a chance to whisper to Philemon. "Well, well, wife," answered Philemon, "you have been walking in a sort of dream. If *I* had poured out the milk I should have seen through it. There was more in the pitcher than you thought, that is all."

And when Quicksilver asked for another cup of the delicious milk, old Philemon himself peeped into the pitcher. It was empty, but all at once Philemon saw a tiny white fountain gush up from the bottom of the pitcher and fill it to the brim.

"Who are ye, wonder-working strangers?" he cried, bewildered.

"Your guests, my good Philemon, and your friends," replied the elder traveler. "And may your pitcher never be empty for kind Baucis and yourself any more than for the needy wayfarer!"

The next morning the guests were early astir. Baucis and Philemon walked with them a short distance. As they looked toward the valley, where, only the day before, they had seen the houses, the gardens, the clumps of trees, and the wide street with children playing in it, they saw instead the broad, blue surface of a lake.

JUPITER
After a bust in the Vatican

"Alas!" cried the kind-hearted people, "what has become of our neighbors?"

"They exist no longer as men and women," said the elder traveler, while a roll of thunder echoed at a distance. "There was no use nor beauty in such a life as theirs. They are transformed to fishes. Look back, friends, at your cottage."

GREECE

They looked back. Instead of the humble cottage a palace of white marble, with wide-open portal, rose before them. "There is your home," said the stranger. "Be as kind to travelers as you were to us last evening."

So Philemon and Baucis lived in the palace and made happy everybody who happened to pass that way, and the miraculous pitcher never became empty.

One day in front of the portal appeared two stately trees with intertwining boughs. One was an oak and the other a linden tree.

"I am old Philemon!" murmured the oak.

"I am old Baucis!" murmured the linden tree.

It was plain that the old couple had renewed their age in these trees. What a hospitable shade did they fling around them! Their leaves whispered ever, "Welcome, traveler, welcome!" Some kind soul built a circular seat round both the trunks, and there the weary and the thirsty used to rest and quaff milk abundantly out of the miraculous pitcher.

Adapted from "A Wonder-Book for Girls and Boys"

Philemon (fĭ lē'mọn). — **Baucis** (bau'sĭs). — **Giovanni da Bologna** (jō-vän'nē dä bō̇ lōn'yä). — **a roll of thunder**: the thunderbolt was the sign of Zeus (zūs), or Jupiter, king of the gods. — **Quicksilver**: Mercury, or Hermes (hẽr'mēz), the messenger of the gods.

THE PARADISE OF CHILDREN

Nathaniel Hawthorne

Long, long ago, when this old world was young, there was a child, named Epimetheus, who had neither father nor mother. So, that he might not be lonely, another child, fatherless and motherless like himself, was sent from a far country, to live with him and be his playfellow and helpmate. Her name was Pandora.

The first thing that Pandora saw, when she entered the cottage where Epimetheus dwelt, was a great box; and almost the first question she asked was this: "Epimetheus, what have you in that box?"

"My dear Pandora," answered Epimetheus, "that is a secret, and you must not ask questions about it. The box was left here to be kept safely, and I do not myself know what it contains."

"But who gave it to you?" asked Pandora. "And where did it come from?"

"That is a secret, too," replied Epimetheus.

"How provoking!" exclaimed Pandora. "I wish the great ugly box were out of the way!"

"Oh, come, don't think of it any more," cried Epimetheus. "Let us run out of doors and play with the other children."

GREECE

In those wonderful days the children never quarreled among themselves; they never cried or sulked. Not one of those things called Troubles had yet been seen on the earth.

But this box in Epimetheus' house began to make a faint shadow of a Trouble in Pandora's heart. "What in the world can be inside of it?" she kept saying to herself and to Epimetheus.

"I wish, Pandora, you would talk about something besides the box," said Epimetheus at last. "Come, let us go and gather some ripe figs for our supper. Let us run out and have a merry time with our playmates."

"I am tired of merry times," answered Pandora. "I think about the box all the time. I insist upon your telling me what is inside of it."

"As I have already said, fifty times over, I do not know!" replied Epimetheus, getting a little vexed. "How, then, can I tell you what is inside?"

"You might open it," said Pandora, looking sideways at Epimetheus, "and then we could see for ourselves."

"Pandora, what are you thinking of?" exclaimed Epimetheus. And his face expressed so much horror at the idea of looking into the box, which had been confided to him on the condition of his never opening it, that Pandora thought it best not to suggest it any more. Still she could not help thinking and talking about the box.

"At least," said she, "you can tell me how it came here."

"It was left at the door," replied Epimetheus, "by a person who looked very smiling and intelligent. He had on a cap that was made partly of feathers, so that it seemed to have wings."

"What sort of a staff had he?" asked Pandora.

"Oh, the most curious staff you ever saw!" cried Epimetheus. "It was like two serpents twisting around a stick, and was carved so naturally that I at first thought the serpents were alive."

"I know him," said Pandora. "It was Quicksilver. He brought me hither, as well as the box. No doubt he intended it for me. Probably it contains pretty dresses for me to wear, or toys for us to play with, or something nice for us both to eat."

"Perhaps so," answered Epimetheus, turning away. "But until Quicksilver comes back and tells us so, we have no right to lift the lid of the box."

"What a dull boy he is!" muttered Pandora, as Epimetheus left the cottage. "I wish he had a little more enterprise."

After Epimetheus had gone, Pandora stood gazing at the box. In spite of her calling it ugly, it was a very handsome article of furniture. It was made of

GREECE

a beautiful kind of wood, with dark, rich veins spreading over its surface, which was so highly polished that Pandora could see her face in it. The edges and corners of the box were carved with the most wonderful skill. It was fastened, not by a lock, but by an intricate knot of gold cord. There appeared to be no end to this knot, and no beginning. Two or three times already Pandora had stooped over the box and taken the knot between her thumb and forefinger, but without positively trying to undo it.

"I really believe," she said to herself, "that I begin to see how it was done. Perhaps I could tie it up again after undoing it. There would be no harm in that, surely. Even Epimetheus would not blame me for that. I need not open the box, and should not, of course, without the foolish boy's consent."

Just then, by the merest accident, she gave the knot a twist, and it untwined itself, as if by magic, and left the box without a fastening.

"This is the strangest thing I ever knew!" said Pandora. "What will Epimetheus say? And how can I possibly tie it up again?"

She made one or two attempts to restore the knot, but soon found it quite beyond her skill.

"Oh," said Pandora, "when Epimetheus finds the knot untied, he will know I did it. How shall I make him believe I have not looked into the box?"

Then a naughty thought came into her heart. Since she would be suspected of looking into the box, she might just as well do so. Oh, very naughty and very foolish Pandora! Then she thought she heard the murmur of small voices within, a little tumult of whispers in her ear: " Let us out, dear Pandora; pray let us out. We will be your playfellows. Only let us out!"

"Is there something alive in the box?" thought Pandora. "Well — yes — I am resolved to take just one little peep!"

Meantime Epimetheus was not as happy as usual out of doors. He was afraid he had been cross to Pandora, so he came back softly, meaning to surprise her. But just as he entered, the naughty Pandora had her hand on the lid and was about to open the mysterious box. If Epimetheus had cried out, she would have stopped and probably the box would never have been opened. But Epimetheus was curious himself; he wanted to know what was in that box. So he was almost as much at fault as she. He kept still and watched.

Pandora raised the lid, and the cottage grew suddenly dark. A swarm of winged creatures brushed past her, flying out of the box. Next she heard Epimetheus crying out in pain, "Oh, I am stung, I am stung! Pandora, why did you open the box?"

Pandora let fall the lid. She saw a crowd of ugly little shapes with bats' wings, and long stings in their tails. Then she began to scream. One had stung her.

Now I must tell you that these ugly things were the whole family of earthly Troubles. They were Cares and Sorrows and Diseases and more kinds of Naughtiness than it would be of any use to talk about. Not one had been in the world until Pandora opened the box.

You can imagine that Pandora and Epimetheus did not want the ugly swarm in their cottage. The first thing they did was to open the doors and windows and let the winged Troubles fly abroad.

Epimetheus sat down sullenly in a corner, with his back toward Pandora. She threw herself on the floor with her head on the box and cried bitterly.

Suddenly there was a gentle little tap on the inside of the lid. "What can that be?" said Pandora, lifting her head. Again the tap! "Who are you?" asked Pandora. "Who are you, inside of this naughty box?"

A sweet little voice spoke from within. "Only lift the lid and you shall see."

"Oh, no," answered Pandora, beginning to sob again, "I have had enough of lifting the lid."

"Ah," said the sweet little voice, "I am not like the naughty creatures with stings in their tails. I am sure you will let me out!"

"Epimetheus, shall I lift the lid?" asked Pandora.

"Just as you please," said Epimetheus. "You have done so much mischief already, you may as well do a little more."

"Ah, naughty boy," cried the little voice, in a laughing tone. "He knows he is longing to see me. Come, dear Pandora, lift up the lid. I am in a hurry to comfort you."

"Epimetheus," exclaimed Pandora, "come what may, I am resolved to open the box!"

"And as the lid seems heavy," cried Epimetheus, running across the room, "I will help you."

The two children lifted the lid. Out flew a sunny and smiling little being, and hovered about the room, throwing a light wherever she went. She flew to Epimetheus and touched with her fingers the spot where the Trouble had stung him, and immediately the pain of it was gone. Then she kissed Pandora on the forehead, and her hurt was cured.

"Pray, who are you, beautiful creature?" asked Pandora.

"I am to be called Hope!" answered the fairy. "I was packed into the box, to make amends for that swarm of ugly Troubles. Never fear! we shall do pretty well in spite of them all."

"Your wings are colored like the rainbow!" exclaimed Pandora. "How very beautiful!"

GREECE

"Yes, they are like the rainbow," said Hope, "because, glad as my nature is, I am made of tears as well as smiles."

"And will you stay with us," asked Epimetheus, "forever and ever?"

"As long as you need me," said Hope, with her pleasant smile, — "and that will be as long as you live in the world, — I promise never to desert you. Yes, dear children, I know something very good and beautiful that is to be given to you some day!"

"Oh, tell us," they exclaimed, "tell us what it is!"

"Do not ask me," replied Hope, putting her finger on her rosy mouth. "But trust in my promise, for it is true."

"We do trust you!" cried Epimetheus and Pandora, both in one breath.

And so they did, and so has everybody trusted Hope, — everybody who has lived in this world, up to this very day.

Adapted from "A Wonder-Book for Girls and Boys"

Epimetheus (ĕp ĭ mē'thūs). — **Pandora** (păn dō'rạ). — **I am made of tears as well as smiles**: a rainbow is produced only when the sun shines through drops of rain.

NORTH PORCH OF THE ERECHTHEUM

PERICLES

Pericles was one of the greatest statesmen the world has seen. He was born in Athens, of noble parentage, more than four hundred years before the Christian era and more than twenty-four hundred years ago. We have learned most about him from the writings of Plutarch, a famous Greek historian who lived five hundred years after Pericles. Pericles was First Citizen of Athens for thirty-one years. The age in which he lived is known in history as the Age of Pericles.

Pericles' first teacher was a man named Anaxagoras, a noble philosopher, gentle and dignified, who gave up all his own property to the state, that he might devote himself to thought. From him Pericles learned a quietness and calmness in all his movements which nothing could disturb, and an even tone of voice which produced the greatest effect on his hearers.

Once, in the market place where he was engaged in important business, he was abused and ill spoken of all day long by a good-for-nothing fellow. Pericles attended to his own business in perfect silence and in the evening went home quietly, the man still dogging him at his heels and pelting him all the way with abusive talk. It was dark by this time, and stepping into the house, Pericles ordered one of his servants to take a torch and go along with the man and see him safe home.

He appeared in public only on great occasions. His speeches were carefully prepared, and before he spoke, he prayed to the gods that not a single unworthy word might escape his lips.

For thirty years he kept peace at home in Athens and persuaded the people to take the money that was left over after they had provided everything necessary for war, and to spend it in making the city beautiful. So it was owing to Pericles that Athens became the most beautiful city in the world — the wonder of the world, Plutarch says.

He himself lived in a modest, simple house. Not a cent of the public money did he ever spend on himself. He had no title but First Citizen, which the Athenians gave him of their own accord.

Perhaps, after all, the most remarkable thing that he did was to make a people who were naturally idle and lazy *want to work*. They thought it a disgrace for a free man to work; work was for slaves. But Pericles persuaded a whole city not only to work but to *love* to work. Temples and theaters and public buildings rose on every hand.

The materials used in this construction were stone, brass, ivory, gold, ebony, and cypress wood. There was need of smiths and carpenters, stonecutters, dyers, workers in brass and bronze and ivory and gold, painters and embroiderers. Merchants and shipmasters carried the goods to Athens, and wagoners, ropemakers, flax workers, shoemakers, road makers, and miners all took hold and helped. For several years everybody worked, carrying stone, tugging and lifting and carving.

Thus the beautiful buildings rose, stately in size and exquisite in form. The workmen strove to outdo one another in beauty of design and workmanship. The wonderful thing was that the work was done so rapidly and so well.

Plutarch tells us that five hundred years after they were finished, these buildings in Athens were not only beautiful and elegant, but in their vigor and freshness looked as if just erected. "There is," Plutarch says, "a sort of bloom of newness upon these works of Pericles, preserving them from the touch of time, as if they had a perennial spirit of life mingled in their composition."

Adapted from Plutarch's "Parallel Lives"

Pericles (pĕr´ĭ klēz). — **Anaxagoras** (ăn ăk săg´ŏ răs).

MOUNT LYCABETTUS FROM THE PARTHENON

THE PARTHENON

Among the beautiful buildings erected by Pericles was the Parthenon, a temple sacred to the goddess Athena. It has been called the most perfect of all the buildings ever erected in the world. It was built on the Acropolis, of white Pentelic marble that has turned a golden color from time, and was completed in 438 B.C. In construction, in sculptured decoration, and in color it embodied the best genius and skill of Athens at the height of her glory.

It stood for more than two thousand years and was used as a Greek temple, then as a Christian church, then as a Mohammedan mosque. Finally, in a war between Turkey and Venice in 1687, the Turks used it as a storehouse for powder. The powder was blown up by a bomb, and more than half the wonderful building was destroyed. The front, though much injured, is still standing and is the most beautiful object in Athens to-day.

Parthenon (pär′thē nŏn). — **Acropolis** (a krŏp′ō lĭs) a citadel, or fortified height, in a Greek city; often used, as in Athens, as a sacred precinct for temples and altars. — **Pentelic** (pĕn tĕl′ĭk): from Mount Pentelicus. — **Lycabettus** (lĭk a bĕt′us).

FRONT OF THE PARTHENON

EARTH PROUDLY WEARS THE PARTHENON

Ralph Waldo Emerson

Earth proudly wears the Parthenon,
As the best gem upon her zone,
And Morning opes with haste her lids
To gaze upon the Pyramids;
O'er England's abbeys bends the sky,
As on its friends, with kindred eye;
For out of thought's interior sphere
These wonders rose to upper air;

GREECE

And Nature gladly gave them place,
Adopted them into her race,
And granted them an equal date
With Andes and with Ararat.

These temples grew as grows the grass;
Art might obey, but not surpass.
The passive Master lent his hand
To the vast soul that o'er him planned;
And the same power that reared the shrine
Bestrode the tribes that knelt within.
Ever the fiery Pentecost
Girds with one flame the countless host, ...
The word by seers or sibyls told,
In groves of oak, or fanes of gold,
Still floats upon the morning wind,
Still whispers to the willing mind.
One accent of the Holy Ghost
The heedless world hath never lost.

Abridged from "The Problem"

zone: girdle. — **abbey**: a monastery or the church of a monastery. — **Pentecost**: see Acts ii. — **sibyls** (sĭb′ĭlz): women supposed to have the gift of foretelling the future.

THE RUINED PARTHENON

Bayard Taylor

Over the ramparts of the Acropolis you see no more of the mountains or the distant Ægean islands; you are on the summit, alone with the Parthenon. You need no pointing finger; your eye turns instinctively to where it stands. Over heaps of ruin, over a plain buried under huge fragments of hewn and sculptured marble — a wilderness of mutilated art — it rises between you and the sky, which forms its only background. Broken down to the earth in the middle, like a ship which has struck and parted, with the roof, cornices, and friezes mostly gone, and not a column unmutilated, and yet with the tawny gold of two thousand years staining its once spotless marble, you doubt for a moment whether the melancholy of its ruin or the perfect and majestic loveliness which shines through that ruin is more powerful.

I did not stop to solve this doubt. Once having looked upon the Parthenon, it was impossible to look elsewhere, and I drew nearer and nearer, finding a narrow lane through the chaos of fragments piled almost as high as my head, until I stood below the western front. I looked up at the Doric shafts,

GREECE

colossal, as befitted the shrine of a goddess, yet tender and graceful as flower stems, upholding without effort the massive entablature and the shattered pediment, and I was seized with an overpowering

THE APPROACH TO THE ACROPOLIS

mixture of the loftiest admiration and of the most unmitigated grief and indignation.

We ascended the steps to the floor of the temple, walked over its barren pavement, past the spot where stood the statue of ivory and gold, to the center, and sat down in the marble chairs of the ancient priests, to contemplate the wreck in silence. Oh, unutterable sorrow! — for all the ages to come can never restore the glory which has here been destroyed. In the perfect symmetry of those wondrous columns was solved the enigma of that harmony which is the very being of God and the operation of his laws. These blocks of sunny marble were piled upon each other to the chorus of the same song which the seasons sing in their ordered round and the planets in their balanced orbits.

After a while my friend desperately said, "I would destroy all the later architecture of Europe, except the Duomo at Milan, to restore this." So, almost, would I. For this is the true temple of Divinity. Its perfect beauty is the expression of love and joy, such as never yet dwelt in the groined arches of Gothic aisles or the painted domes of Roman worship. God has no better temple on earth than the Parthenon.

Abridged from " Travels in Greece "

Doric (dŏr'ĭk) **shaft**: a type of pillar distinguished for simplicity and strength. — **entablature**: the layers of horizontal work between the tops of the columns and the eaves. — **statue of ivory and gold**: a statue of Athena, made by Phidias (fĭd'ĭ ạs), the great Greek sculptor, and placed in the Parthenon. — **Duomo** (dwŏ'mō) **at Milan** (mĭl'ạn): the cathedral at Milan, Italy, by some considered to be the finest cathedral in Europe. — **groined arch**: a curve made by two intersecting arches. — **Gothic aisles**: aisles overspanned by the high and sharply pointed arches common to many Christian churches.

THE ACROPOLIS RESTORED

IN ARCADY

(To Henry C. Bunner)

ROBERT LOUIS STEVENSON

You know the way to Arcady
Where I was born;
You have been there, and fain
Would there return.
Some that go thither bring with them
Red rose or jeweled diadem
As secrets of the secret king;
I, only what a child would bring.
Yet I do think my song is true;
For this is how the children do;
This is the tune to which they go
In sunny pastures high and low;
The treble pipes not otherwise
Sing daily under sunny skies
In Arcady the dear;
And you who have been there before,
And love that country evermore,
May not disdain to hear.

Arcady (är′ka̧ dĭ): a poetical name for Arcadia in Greece, used to indicate a place of simple, innocent pleasure. See Bunner's poem, "The Way to Arcady." — **treble pipes**: a wind instrument consisting of three long tubes. — **Hermes** (hēr′mēz): the Greek name of Mercury. — **Praxiteles** (prăk sĭt′ê lēz).

THE HERMES OF PRAXITELES
After the statue at Olympia

SPRINGTIME IN GREECE

George Horton

This extract is from a book descriptive of country life in modern Greece, written by a former United States minister to Greece. Mr. Horton describes a summer spent by his family at Poros, a country village on the seashore near Athens.

Our daily walk to market led through the lemon orchard to the back gate of the garden, whence a narrow lane conducted us to the little town of Galata, where one crosses over to Poros in a rowboat. It was scarcely a mile, but we were fully two hours walking it the first day, the wild flowers made such children of us. It was in early March, when the air is soft in Greece and the fields are fresh and green. The gardeners were digging up the fresh earth and were setting out tomato and lettuce plants, — not the little stringy heads of lettuce that we eat in America, but a tall, crisp variety that you break off leaf by leaf and crunch like asparagus.

The garden path was lined with peach, pear, almond, and apricot trees, and these were all in bloom. One young tree especially delighted us. It was slender and graceful as a young girl, and its leaves were completely hidden under immense snowy blossoms which, when you looked close, betrayed a delicate tinge of pink.

The bees too were at work. Who calls them when the flowers are ready? Tennyson has told us about the bees. They play the same lyre in Greece as in England, and they strum its drowsy strings to-day just as they did thousands of years ago.

"And murmuring of innumerable bees!" Greece is the bees' reveling ground. We had been in the country three years before we learned how to procure Hymettus honey *ad libitum*, although we had tasted the genuine article after a week's residence in Athens. It happened thus: As I was walking along the street one day I met a shepherd carrying a pine limb to which was attached a huge triangular comb of yellow honey. I bought it from him and took it triumphantly home. I gave the man. I forget how many drachmas, but that first taste of real Hymettus honey was worth dollars instead of drachmas to me.

For two years after meeting that shepherd the Kyria and I used to watch the silver slopes of old Hymettus and wonder where the famous honey came from in the ancient days. I explained to her frequently that trees grew there more thickly then than now, and that in consequence many small streams formerly trickled down ravines that have long since become dry. "The bees too are gone,"

I said, and this idea was corroborated by our frequent attempts to buy Hymettus honey in the shops. We were told that a firm in Piræus had the monopoly of the real product and sold it to the English ships. I bought a tin, but it was no more like the nectar of my triangle of the pine bough than "golden drips" resembles maple sugar.

Again we were informed that one Merlin of Athens had bought the entire crop, which he sold in small tins at an enormous price. One trial was sufficient; all the rest was left for the innocent tourists, who paid the belated wizard a large profit on his ingenious outlay.

It remained for an angry bee to enlighten me, and to teach me that the Greece of the bucolic poets is not yet entirely dead. One May evening we were hurrying across a wild-thyme field, at the foot of Mount Hymettus, to catch the car for town, when a bee suddenly fastened his stinger in my eyelid and hung there buzzing. Of course I was angry at the time, but after the wound ceased aching I began to think, with the result that we made another trip in the same direction a day or two afterwards. A little inquiry brought us to the bee country proper. We found rows and rows of hives at the foot of a cliff on the mountain side, and a dozen or so of rustic villagers on guard. These hives we had seen

GREECE

a hundred times before, but had not recognized them, as they were simply conical baskets, and looked, at a little distance, for all the world like rocks.

We bought about thirty pounds direct from the hives, and I have no hesitation in declaring it the best and most wholesome honey in the world. There is no way of describing the taste of it, save to say that it tastes exactly as wild thyme smells. From the countrymen we learned that there are thousands of acres of wild thyme all about the mountain.

The sun was setting that day as we left the hives and cut across to the main road through the wild-thyme fields. The bees were just coming home, and we soon found ourselves in the center of a cloud of them. The air was utterly still, but they drifted obliquely by, as though floating on a gentle breeze. One of the countrymen shouted, " Don't move, and they won't touch you!" So we stood still and watched them. I do not know whether the little insects themselves were so yellow, or whether it was the setting sun that shone through the long cloud as it drifted by, but I could not help thinking of the line in the poem, " Swarms of tawny bees."

But all this is about Mount Hymettus and its famous honey, and we have forgotten that we are down in the Peloponnesus by the seashore and on our way through a lemon grove to the Poros market.

As we strolled slowly along toward the market, the Kyria and I, we stopped now and then to listen to the bass-viol boom of some large, iridescent green beetles. The poppies were blazing with their reddest flame, plashing the green wheat with frequent patches of blood-red. A tiny beetle buzzed in every poppy's heart.

In the early flush and triumph of the Greek spring the green of the wheat is so vivid, and the red of the poppies so fiery, that the peaceful hillsides seem to have arrayed themselves in barbaric splendor. In March the poppies begin to bloom, and they are in full revel by the middle of April. Then you see them everywhere,— in the fields and country lanes and even atop of the mud fences, where they have gallantly leaped in their onward march.

But I do not think one gains most pleasure in Greece from the poppies, splendid as they are. The anemones hold rival sway in that land. Whoever sowed the poppy seeds mixed therewith an equal quantity of delicately tinted windflowers. And of all places in Greece, or perhaps in the world, they grow thickest on the field of Marathon.

There are many tiny wild flowers too in Greece, that hide among the grass and are so exquisitely beautiful that one understands why they could not have been larger without sacrificing something of their daintiness. I think we were most pleased, on that first trip to market, by certain tiny four-pointed stars of dark blue, with a yellow eye in the center. There were millions of them, and all among them other stars of the same shape and size, terra cotta in color; besides these, dandelions, buttercups, white daisies, and occasionally patches of yellow daisies — yellow and gold.

Asphodel! acres and acres of it, on the hillside. We walked among it hand in hand and imagined ourselves happy shades, far from all the cares and anxieties of life. Waist-deep in asphodel, that swayed gently in a breeze from the near-by sea, we waded. Pale pink were the waxen flowers we plucked, and without perfume, like a beautiful body without a soul.

This is a stately plant, as befits the symbol of death, for it stands up tall and straight, with stalks that branch out symmetrically from the main stem. The plain where it grows seems a great table set with many silver candelabra.

We came suddenly, at the farther side of a little knoll, into a field all life and light and color, — a lawn of grass, closely cropped and brilliantly interwoven with white and yellow daisies, bluebells, and poppies.

"Hear the bees!" cried the Kyria. Stooping down, I found that every blossom was held by a buzzing insect.

How easy it must have been for the ancient Greeks to think in poetry! Paganism adapted itself so easily to the impressions of nature and to the imaginings of æsthetic and susceptible minds. Coming over that little knoll, I felt like Orpheus when he emerged from Hades and stood for a moment blinking at the sunny world.

Abridged from "In Argolis"

Poros (pô′rŏs). — **Galata** (gä′lä tä). — "**And murmuring of innumerable bees**": quoted from Tennyson's poem, "The Princess." — **ad libitum** (ăd lĭb′ĭ tụm): Latin for "at will," "as much as we liked." — **Kyria** (kē rē′ạ): the Greek word for "lady"; used here as the author's name for his wife. — "**golden drips**": an imitation of maple sugar. — **belated wizard**: here, one having the same name as Merlin, the famous wizard of King Arthur's time, but living long afterward. — **bucolic** (bụ kŏl′ĭk): relating to the life of a shepherd; hence, pastoral, rustic. — **Peloponnesus** (pĕl ō pọ nē′sụs): the southern peninsula of Greece. — **anemone** (ạ nĕm′ō nē): windflower. — **Marathon** (măr′ạ thŏn): a plain east of Athens. — **asphodel** (ăs′fō dĕl): a blossom of the lily kind; in Greek mythology the plant of the blessed dead, its pale blossoms covering the meadows of Hades (hā′dēz), the abode of the dead. — **candelabra** (kăn dē lā′brạ): branched candlesticks. — **Orpheus** (ôr′fūs): the musician who, the poets said, could make all animals, and even trees and stones, follow him when he played on his lyre. — **Argolis** (är′gŏ lĭs).

A MODERN NAUSICAA

George Horton

Nausicaa passed here yesterday, seated astride of a donkey. She was neatly dressed in blue homespun, and her sister sat behind her, directly over the animal's hind legs. Her mother, a wholesome-looking peasant woman, was walking and driving another donkey laden with a great mountain of soiled linen and other wearing apparel. An enormous copper kettle, bound to one side of the mountain, blazed intolerably except for its blackened bottom. The little caravan was on its way to Heftamyloi, or Seven Mills, to do a washing that had been collecting during — no one knows how long. There are many gushing springs at Heftamyloi, which is situated high up in the hills. These springs furnish power for several old-fashioned water mills, where the farmers take their grain to be ground.

Every man has moments when he is discontented with his lot, when he dreams that he should like to be something as widely different as possible from what he is, — an Arab sheik, for instance, dwelling in a tent in the desert; a South Sea trader, captain of a pearling vessel; or the Grand Lama of Lassa. When I have the blues, I sometimes wish I were the Sultan of Sulu, and at other times that I were those millers up there in the mountains of Argolis. The air they drink is champagne of a most divine blending — sea breeze and mountain breeze. The waters sing to them and work for them, so that they have nothing to do but sit in the shade of the great platane trees and look down upon the rest of the world. Silver-white olive orchards, red plowed fields, molten gleaming seas, purple islands, are all spread out below them like a mighty panorama. The miller sees the ships, their sails no bigger than pocket handkerchiefs, come into the harbor; he watches them open their wings and fly away, but he asks not whence they come or whither they go. He is as indifferent to the cares of men as were the happy gods. There is room in his soul for no other voice than the eternal pouring of the waters and the purring of the millstones.

To this beautiful spot the maidens of the surrounding country bring the family washing every month or so — an expedition that is often more of a picnic than a hard day's work. I never see a mountain of soiled clothing trotting by on the four legs of a donkey, that I do not think of Nausicaa. Change the donkey into a lofty chariot drawn by mules, and the peasant woman into a princess and her beautiful attendants, and there you are.

GREECE

I could spare any passage of equal length out of the poets, rather than that Homeric dream of the Phæacian isles. What a glorious old socialist Homer must have been at heart, despite the fact that he made his living by singing of the prowess of the nobility. Was ever labor more ingenuously and more heartfully glorified than in that incident of

THE ACROPOLIS AND THE TEMPLE OF JUPITER

Nausicaa? In Homer's ideal community the king's daughter helps with the family washing as a matter of course, and she rejoices in her task. And labor goes hand in hand with play to such an extent that you hardly realize when the work ends and the sport begins. For after those beautiful girls had put the garments into the tubs and had trodden them clear with their white feet, they spread them out upon the shining sands to dry; then they disported in the river like nymphs, and ate their lunch with much chattering, no doubt, and no end of silvery laughter, after which they played at ball, and Nausicaa led them in song. In mentioning that game of ball, old Homer does not fail to speak of the participants as "white-armed," and that one adjective brings the whole graceful, lovely, æsthetic, joyous tableau up before us: the princess, most beautiful where all are fair, the flying draperies, the lithe movements and unconscious classic poses, the little river, the seashore, and the sea.

Abridged from " In Argolis "

Heftamyloi (hĕf tä′mē lē). — **Grand Lama** (lä′mạ) **of Lassa** (läs′ä): the supreme pontiff of an order of Buddhist (bŏŏd′ĭst) monks living in Lassa, the capital of Tibet (tĭ bĕt′). — **Sultan of Sulu** (sōō lōō′): Lord of the Sulu Islands, an archipelago in the Philippines. — **platane** (plăt′ăn): plane tree.

THE BOOK[1]

Emily Dickinson

There is no frigate like a book
    To take us leagues away,
Nor any coursers like a page
    Of prancing poetry.
This traverse may the poorest take
    Without oppress of toll;
How frugal is the chariot
    That bears a human soul!

frigate: sailing vessel. — **coursers**: horses. — **traverse**: crossing, journey. — **frugal**: economical, inexpensive.

[1] From "Poems" by Emily Dickinson; copyright, 1896, by Roberts Brothers.

ANCIENT ITALY
After the painting by J. M. W. Turner

ROME

THE FLIGHT OF ÆNEAS

Translated by Harlan H. Ballard

This is a selection from the "Æneid," the most famous of ancient Latin poems. Æneas is the mythical hero who, after fleeing from Troy and undergoing many adventures, lands in Italy and lays the foundations of the great Roman Empire.

After long years of siege Troy has fallen into the hands of the Greeks, and Æneas, escaping from the tumult, hastens to his home and begs his aged father, Anchises, with his wife and little son, to flee with him. Anchises at first refuses, saying he has no desire to live if Troy has fallen. Æneas, seeing that Anchises will not listen to him, calls for his armor, that he may make one more hopeless attempt to avenge his country.

Then, again girded with steel, I fitted my arm to my buckler,
Ready to rush with the speed of despair from the door of the palace.
Lo, however, my wife, arresting my feet at the threshold,
Clung to my knees, holding out to his father our little Iulus.

"If thou art bent upon death, take us with thee
    wherever thou goest;
But, if thou hast any reason to trust in the arms
    thou hast taken,
First defend this home. Who will care for our little
    Iulus?
Who for thy father? And whom has thy once
    honored wife to protect her?"
Shrieking these words aloud, she filled the whole
    house with her wailing,
When, to our wonderment, rises before us a marvellous omen;
For, while tenderly kissed and caressed by his sorrowing parents,
Lo! a light tongue of fire appears on the head of Iulus,
Shedding a lambent light, and a flame, quite gentle
    and harmless,
Kisses his curly hair and plays about on his forehead.
Startled, and trembling with fear, we hasten to rescue
    our darling,
Shaking his blazing hair, and quenching the flame
    at the fountain.

   Father Anchises, however, uplifting his eyes to
    the heavens,
Joyously stretched his hands to the sky, and made
    his petition:

ROME

"Jupiter, lord of all, if prayers are ever availing,
Look thou upon us; we ask no more; and, if we
    are worthy,
Then, O Father, vouchsafe thine aid, and second
    this omen!"
Scarce had the old man spoken these words, when,
    suddenly pealing,
Thundered the left, and a star rushed down from
    the sky through the darkness,
Drawing a glittering train, and passing in terrible
    splendor.
Then, after gliding high o'er the roof of the palace,
    we saw it
Bury itself, unquenched, in the depths of the forest
    of Ida,
Ploughing a flaming way, and then the long track
    of its furrow
Blazes, and far and wide the mountain is smoking
    with sulphur.

  Then, indeed, overcome, my father slowly arising,
Speaks to the gods in prayer, and blesses the star
    they have sent him.
"Now, no longer delay! wherever thou leadest, I
    follow.
Gods of my fathers, protect my home, watch over
    my grandson!

Yours is the augury; Troy is still in your merciful
   keeping.
Yes, I yield, and now, my son, lead on and I follow."

   Yet, as he speaks, even now, through the town
      the fire is more clearly
Heard, and the billows of flame are rolling nearer
   and nearer.
"Come then, father belovèd, behold, my neck is thy
   refuge!
See! my shoulders I bend; such freight is no weari-
   some burden.
Be the event as it may, our share of the danger is
   equal;
Equal our share of hope; now, closely let little Iulus
Cling to my side, and my wife coming after shall
   follow our footsteps.
You, my servants, to what I shall say give closest
   attention:
There is a hill as you pass from the town, and a
   temple of Ceres,
Old and disused; and a tree, an old cypress, is
   standing beside it:
Following different paths, we shall meet in this
   common asylum.
Father, thy hand must be charged with our sacred
   emblems and hearth-gods;

THE FLIGHT OF ÆNEAS
After the painting by Raphael

I, coming forth from so frightful a war, still reeking
    with slaughter,
Dare not approach them now; nor before in a free-
    flowing fountain
I shall have bathed." . . .

    Thus having spoken, my bended neck and the
    breadth of my shoulders
Covering o'er with a cloak and the tawny skin of a
    lion,
Under my burden I rise; at my right our little Iulus
Twines his hand in mine, and strives to keep step
    with his father;
Follows my wife behind, and we hasten along through
    the shadows.
Me, whom, an hour before, no rain of weapons had
    daunted,
No, nor the Greeks, though rolling against us in
    serried battalions,
Now each breeze dismayed, each sound now filled
    with disquiet,
Hesitant, doubly afraid for the charge of my hand
    and my shoulders.

                                From Vergil's Æneid

Æneid (ē nē′ĭd): the story of the adventures of Æneas. — **Anchises** (ăn kī′sēz). — **Iulus** (ī ū′lus). — **omen** : that which foretells some future event. — **Ida** (ī′da̱): a mountain near ancient Troy. — **Raphael** (răf′å ĕl).

THE SIBYLLINE BOOKS

Tarquinius Superbus
  In ancient Rome held sway,
With cruel might he urged his course
  And none dared say him nay.
Before his palace gates there came
  One day a woman old
With streaming hair and dark gray robes,
  Her gaze both stern and bold.
Nine books of ponderous weight she bore
  Close pressed against her breast;
To see the king was her demand.
  And lo! at her behest
Tarquinius came. His haughtiness
  Was mirrored back in truth.
" 'T is well thou heed'st the Sibyl's call,"
  She said; " the gods, forsooth,
Have trusted to these sacred rolls
  The destiny of Rome;
For thirty golden coins they 're thine.
  From my far distant home,
From Cumæ have I come for this."
  The king with high disdain
Refused the proffered rolls and turned
  Him to his way again.

Straight from the palace gate she passed,
    Her wild locks flying free,
Three rolls she burned, then came once more
    And offered mockingly
The six books left, the price the same.
    The king with darkening eye,

THE CUMÆAN SIBYL
After the painting by Elihu Vedder

With rising rage behind his scorn,
    Again refused to buy.
Once more three books she burned, again
    Returned with only three,
Demanding still the thirty coins.
    What solemn mystery

ROME

Lay hid behind this strange demand?
　No mockery now! No rage!
The augurs, summoned in swift haste,
　Explored the sacred page.
" O king," said they, " thou hast put by
　The gods' great gift to thee;
Buy, buy at any price these rolls!"
　The Tarquin silently
Within the Sibyl's lean gray hand
　Pressed thirty coins of gold.
No more within Rome's ancient walls,
　Within the palace old,
Was seen that weird and stooping form,
　That wild and haggard face;
And no man cared what wilderness
　Might be her dwelling place.

Deep in a chest of heavy stone,
　Beneath the temple dome
Which Tarquin's father had upreared
　Upon that hill of Rome
Where since the Capitol hath stood,
　The Sibyl's books were stored;
Two men detailed to guard them there,
　To stand with ready sword —
The Keepers of the Sacred Books,
　The city's priceless hoard.

And as the years rolled on their course,
  When dangers neared the State,
When pestilence and earthquake shock
  Made Rome bewail her fate,
The guidance of the Sacred Books
  The Fathers meekly sought,
Rejoicing if the chosen words
  With helpfulness were fraught.
But when no message could be found
  And death itself seemed nigh,
The six burned books like wraiths of doom
  Their hoary heads reared high,
Seeming to smite with deep reproach,
  With bitter, keen disdain
The land to which such offerings
  Had once been made in vain.

Sibylline (sĭb′ĭ lĭn): pertaining to the sibyls. — **Tarquinius Superbus** (tär kwĭn′ĭ ŭs sŭ pẽr′bŭs): Tarquin the Proud, the last king of ancient Rome, driven out by Brutus, an ancestor of the Brutus who killed Cæsar. — **Cumæ** (kū′mē): an ancient city on the western coast of Italy, near Naples. — **augurs**: Roman officers supposed to be able to foretell future events. — **Fathers**: Roman senators.

THE TEMPLE OF CASTOR AND POLLUX

Isabel Lovell

One evening, although the twilight was fast darkening into night, the Forum of Rome was full of people. Men were talking together in anxious groups; magistrates were holding long consultations; for the army had gone out to battle against their exiled king, Tarquin the Proud, and that day there had been a hard fight at Lake Regillus, not many leagues from Rome.

Close by the temple of Vesta was a spring that belonged, it is said, to the nymph Juturna, and so pure and clear were these waters that they were believed to bring healing to mankind. Near this fountain there suddenly appeared a most surprising sight. Before the people stood two noble knights, whose steeds, all flecked with foam, were drinking from the sacred spring. The armor of these strangers gleamed brightly in the dusk, although they had the air of those that had not only ridden far and fast but also battled long and hard. In awed tones the news of their arrival passed from man to man, until all that were in the Forum had gathered about the youths, who, unmindful of the multitude, continued to refresh themselves and their pure white chargers with the sparkling waters. However, when every one had drawn near, the splendid strangers stood up side by side and, as with a single voice, spoke to the spellbound people, saying: " Hail, men of Rome! Let your hearts be uplifted. From Lake Regillus do we come and would have you know that Tarquin is vanquished and that Rome's standards are planted in his camp. Right valiant has been the fight, for the cause of Rome has this day been defended by the favor of the gods."

Having thus spoken, the glistening knights remounted their noble steeds, quieting them by calling their names in gentle tones — " Ho, Kanthus! " " Now then, good Cyllaros! " — and the voice of these knights was like the sound of deep, sweet music. Then, with a gesture of farewell, they gave rein to their horses, rounded the road by the Temple of Vesta, and were gone!

No trace of the mysterious riders could be found, and a wonderment, almost a fear, seized upon the people in the very midst of their rejoicings. Some murmured that the knights had been but a vision; others declared that these had been no earthly visitors, but Castor and Pollux, twin sons of Jupiter, who had brought the good news to the Roman people.

With the next morning's light there came a messenger in haste from the Roman camp, bearing a

RUINS OF THE TEMPLE OF CASTOR AND POLLUX

strange report. This message was wrapped in leaves of laurel, as was the custom of victorious generals when informing the Senate of a conquest, and in the letter were words proving that in very truth the sons of Jupiter had fought for Rome, for at a moment when the Romans were hard pressed and their courage grew faint, two knights on pure white steeds had suddenly appeared among the foremost ranks. Before them Tarquin's army had fallen back in great confusion, and soon the victory was with the knights of Rome. Upon this the two strange knights had disappeared. Then all knew that the contest had been gained by the favor of the gods and not by the strength of man, and immediately, upon the battlefield, a temple had been vowed to the Twin Brothers, in gratitude for their valiant aid.

A few years later a temple to Castor and Pollux was built in the Forum, just on the spot where the heavenly visitors announced the good news to the people. Statues of the Twin Brothers were later placed in the temple and were always kept in perfect order and repair.

Abridged from "Stories in Stone from the Roman Forum"

Castor (kăs′tẽr). — **Pollux** (pŏl′ŭks). — **Forum** (fō′rum). — **Regillus** (rē̆ jĭl′us). — **Juturna** (jū tûr′na̤). — **Cyllaros** (sĭl′a̤ rŏs).

THE BATTLE OF LAKE REGILLUS

Thomas Babington Macaulay

Sempronius Atratinus
   Sate in the Eastern Gate,
Beside him were three Fathers,
   Each in his chair of state. . . .
And all around the portal,
   And high above the wall,
Stood a great throng of people,
   But sad and silent all;
Young lads, and stooping elders
   That might not bear the mail,
Matrons with lips that quivered,
   And maids with faces pale.

Since the first gleam of daylight,
   Sempronius had not ceased
To listen for the rushing
   Of horse-hoofs from the east.
The mist of eve was rising,
   The sun was hastening down,
When he was aware of a princely pair
   Fast pricking towards the town.
So like they were, man never
   Saw twins so like before;

Red with gore their armour was,
  Their steeds were red with gore.

" Hail to the great Asylum!
  Hail to the hill-tops seven!
Hail to the fire that burns for aye,
  And the shield that fell from heaven!
This day, by Lake Regillus,
  Under the Porcian height,
All in the lands of Tusculum
  Was fought a glorious fight.
To-morrow your Dictator
  Shall bring in triumph home
The spoils of thirty cities
  To deck the shrines of Rome!"

Then burst from that great concourse
  A shout that shook the towers,
And some ran north, and some ran south,
  Crying, " The day is ours!"
But on rode these strange horsemen,
  With slow and lordly pace;
And none who saw their bearing
  Durst ask their name or race.
On rode they to the Forum,
  While laurel-boughs and flowers,
From house-tops and from windows,

ROME

Fell on their crests in showers.
When they drew nigh to Vesta,
　They vaulted down amain,
And washed their horses in the well
　That springs by Vesta's fane.

TEMPLE OF VESTA IN ROME

And straight again they mounted,
　And rode to Vesta's door;
Then, like a blast, away they passed,
　And no man saw them more.
And all the people trembled,
　And pale grew every cheek;
And Sergius the High Pontiff

Alone found voice to speak:
" The gods who live for ever
　Have fought for Rome to-day!
These be the Great Twin Brethren
　To whom the Dorians pray.
Back comes the Chief in triumph,
　Who, in the hour of fight,
Hath seen the Great Twin Brethren
　In harness on his right. . . .
Wherefore they washed their horses
　In Vesta's holy well,
Wherefore they rode to Vesta's door,
　I know, but may not tell.
Here, hard by Vesta's temple,
　Build we a stately dome
Unto the Great Twin Brethren
　Who fought so well for Rome.
And when the months returning
　Bring back this day of fight,
The proud Ides of Quintilis,
　Marked evermore with white,
Unto the Great Twin Brethren
　Let all the people throng,
With chaplets and with offerings,
　With music and with song;
And let the doors and windows
　Be hung with garlands all,

ROME

And let the Knights be summoned
    To Mars without the wall:
Thence let them ride in purple
    With joyous trumpet-sound,
Each mounted on his war-horse,
    And each with olive crowned;
And pass in solemn order
    Before the sacred dome,
Where dwell the Great Twin Brethren
    Who fought so well for Rome!"

Abridged from " Lays of Ancient Rome."

Sempronius Atratinus (sĕm prō'nĭ us ăt ra tī'nus): an appointed consul, or chief magistrate, left in charge of Rome when the regular consuls went to battle. — **sate**: sat. — **Asylum; hill-tops seven**: Rome, built on seven hills. — **the fire that burns for aye**: the sacred fire kept burning in the temple of Vesta, goddess of the hearth. This temple, which stood in the Forum, is now in ruins. The illustration shows a temple of Vesta which stands in another part of Rome. — **the shield that fell from heaven**: tradition says that in the time of Numa Pompilius (nū'ma pŏm pĭl'ĭ us), one of the earliest kings of Rome, a shield fell from heaven, and that Numa had eleven shields made like it, and appointed twelve youths to guard the twelve shields in the temple of Mars. — **Porcian** (pôr'shan) **height**: a hill near Lake Regillus, east of Rome. — **Tusculum** (tŭs'cû lŭm): the country east of Rome. — **Dictator**: commander of the Roman state and army, appointed in time of special danger. — **Sergius** (sẽr'jĭ us). — **the High Pontiff**: the high priest. — **The ... Ides** (īdz) **of Quintilis** (kwĭn tĭ'lĭs): the fifteenth of July. In the ancient Roman calendar the ides of the month were the fifteenth of March, May, July, and October, and the thirteenth of the other months. The first month of the Roman year was March. The fifth month, our July, was called Quintilis, the Latin word for "fifth" being *quintus*. — **Mars without the wall**: the Field of Mars without the city wall, where the troops were drilled.

CROSSING THE RUBICON

William Stearns Davis

Cæsar's brilliant victories in Gaul had opened that province to the Romans. Pompey, the second greatest Roman of his day, was serving as consul in Rome and was watching jealously the growing reputation of his great rival. He broke openly with Cæsar and attached himself to the old aristocratic party. Cæsar now demanded the consulship, knowing that because of the jealousy of his enemies his life would not be safe in Rome without the security of that office. The senate, acting by the orders of these enemies, issued a decree that he should resign as proconsul, or governor, of Gaul and disband his legions by a stated day. That crisis had now come.

On the next day Cæsar called before him the thirteenth legion, the only force he had at Ravenna, and from a pulpit in front of the prætorium he told them the story of what had happened at Rome — of how the senate had outraged the tribunes of the plebs, whom even the violent Sulla had respected. Then Curio, just arrived, declaimed with indignant fervor against the violence and fury of the consuls and Pompeius, and when he concluded, the veterans could restrain their ardor and devotion no longer. Five thousand martial throats roared forth an oath of fealty, and as many swords were waved on high in mad defiance of the senate and the Magnus.

It was a great personal triumph for Cæsar. He stood receiving the plaudits, and repaying with a few gracious words or smiles each protestation of loyalty. Drusus, who was standing behind the proconsul, beside Curio, realized that never before had he seen such outgoing of magnetism and personal energy from man to man, one mind holding in vassalage five thousand. Yet it was all very quickly over. Almost while the plaudits of the centuries were rending the air, Cæsar turned to the senior tribune of the legion.

"Are your men ready for the march, officer?"

The soldier instantly fell into rigid military pose. "Ready this instant, Imperator. We have expected the order."

"March to Ariminum and take possession of the town. March rapidly."

The tribune saluted and stepped back among his cohort, and, as if some conjurer had flourished a wand of magic, in the twinkling of an eye the first century had formed in marching order; every legionary had flung over his shoulder his shield and pack, and at the harsh blare of the military trumpet the whole legion fell into line.

Drusus at once saw that everything was ready for departure. By nightfall it was evident that the proconsul intended to waste no time in starting. Cæsar's words were terse and to the point. "Curio, you will find a fast horse awaiting you. Take it. Ride at full speed after the legion. Take command of the rear cohorts and of the others as you come up with them. Lead rapidly to Ariminum."

And Curio, who was a man of few words when few were needed, saluted and disappeared in the darkness. Drusus followed the general out of the prætorium.

Cæsar motioned to Drusus to sit beside him in the carriage. Antiochus clambered upon the front seat. The autumn season was well advanced. The day, however, had been warm. The night was sultry. There were no stars above, no moon, no wind. A sickening miasmal odor rose from the low, flat country sloping off toward the Adriatic — the smell of overripe fruit, of decaying vegetation, of the harvest grown old. There had been a drought, and now the dust rose thick and heavy, making the mules and travelers cough and the latter cover their faces. Out of the darkness came not the least sound save the creaking of the dead boughs on trees whose dim tracery could just be distinguished against the somber background of the sky.

No one spoke. How long Drusus drifted on in reverie he could not say. Perhaps he fell asleep. A cry from Antiochus startled him out of his stupor. He stared about. It was pitch dark. Antiochus was bawling, "The lantern has jolted out!"

To relight it, in an age when friction matches were unknown, was practically impossible. The only thing to be done was to wait in the road until the morning, or until the moon broke out through the clouds.

"Drusus," remarked the proconsul, "you are the youngest. Can your eyes make out anything to tell us where we are?"

The young man yawned, shook off his drowsiness, and stared out into the gloomy void.

"I can just make out that to our left are tall trees, and I imagine a thicket."

"Very good. If you can see as much as that here, it is safe to proceed. Let us change places, Antiochus. I will take the reins. Do you, Drusus, come and direct me."

Cæsar took the reins and went off at a furious pace. Drusus speedily found that the general's vision was far more keen than his own. Indeed, although the road, he knew, was rough and crooked, they met with no mishaps. Presently a light could be seen twinkling in the distance.

"We must get a guide," remarked the imperator decisively. They at last approached a small farmhouse, where they aroused the countrymen. As a result Antiochus resumed the reins and sped away with a lantern and a stupid peasant boy at his side.

But more misfortune was in store. Barely a mile had they traversed before an ominous crack proclaimed the splitting of an axletree. The cheap hired vehicle could go no farther.

" 'T is a sure sign the gods are against our proceeding this night," expostulated Antiochus; " let us walk back to the farmhouse, my lord."

Cæsar did not deign to give him an answer. He deliberately descended and clasped his pænula over his shoulders. Again the proconsul was all resources. With almost omniscience he led his companions through blind mazes of fallow land and stubble fields, came upon a brook at the only point where there appeared to be any stepping-stones, and at length, just as the murky clouds seemed about to lift, and the first beams of the moon struggled out into the black chaos, the wanderers saw a multitude of fires twinkling before them and knew that they had come upon the rear cohort of the thirteenth legion on its way to Ariminum.

Cæsar skirted the sleeping camp and soon came out again on the highroad. There was a faint paleness in the east; a single lark sang from out the mist of gray ether overhead; an ox of the baggage train rattled his tethering chain and bellowed. A soft, damp river fog touched Drusus's face. Suddenly an early horseman, coming at a moderate

ROME

gallop, was heard down the road. In the stillness the pounding of his steed crept slowly nearer and nearer; then, as he was almost on them, came the hollow clatter of the hoofs upon the planks of a bridge. Cæsar stopped. Drusus felt himself clutched by the arm so tightly that the grasp almost meant pain.

"Do you hear? Do you see?" muttered the imperator's voice in his ear. "The bridge — the river — we have reached it!"

"Your excellency — " began Drusus, sorely at a loss.

"No compliments; this is the Rubicon, the boundaries of Cisalpine Gaul and Italy. On this side I am still the proconsul — not as yet rightly deposed. On the other, Cæsar the outlaw, the insurgent, the enemy of his country, whose hand is against every man, every man's hand against him. What say you? Speak! speak quickly! Shall I cross? Shall I turn back?"

"Imperator," said the young man, struggling to collect his wits and realize the gravity of his own words, "if you did not intend to cross, why send the legion over to commence the invasion? Why harangue them if you had no test to place upon their loyalty?"

"Because," was his answer, "I would not through my own indecision throw away my chance to strike.

But the troops can be recalled. It is not too late. No blood has been shed. I am merely in a position to strike if so I decide. No; nothing is settled."

The light was growing stronger every moment, though the mist still hung heavy and dank. Below their feet the slender stream — it was the end of the season — ran with a monotonous gurgle, now and then casting up a little fleck of foam as it rolled by a small bowlder in its bed.

"Imperator," said Drusus, while Cæsar pressed his hand tighter and tighter, "why advise with an inexperienced young man like myself? Why did you send Curio away? I have no wisdom to offer, nor dare proffer it if such I had."

"Quintus Drusus," replied Cæsar, sinking rather wearily down upon the dry, dying grass, "if I had needed the counsel of a soldier, I should have waited until Marcus Antonius arrived; if I had needed that of a politician, I was a fool to send away Curio; if I desire the counsel of one who is, as yet, neither a man of the camp nor a man of the Forum, but who can see things with clear eyes, can tell what may be neither glorious nor expedient, but what will be the will —" and here the imperator hesitated — "the will of the gods, tell me to whom I shall go."

Drusus was silent; the other continued: "Listen, Quintus Drusus. I do not believe in blind fate. We were not given wills only to have them broken. The function of a limb is not to be maimed, nor severed from the body; a limb is to serve a man. Just so a man and his actions are to serve the ends of a power higher and nobler than he. If he refuse to serve that power, he is like the mortifying limb — a thing of evil to be cut off. And this is true of all of us; we all have some end to serve; we are not created for no purpose." Cæsar paused. When he began again, it was in a different tone of voice. "I have brought you with me because I know you are intelligent, are humane, love your country, and can make sacrifices for her; because you are my friend and to a certain extent share my destiny; because you are too young to have become overprejudiced or calloused to pet foibles and transgressions. Therefore I took you with me, having put off the final decision to the last possible instant. And now I desire your counsel."

"How can I counsel peace!" replied Drusus, warming to a sense of the situation. "Is not Italy in the hand of tyrants? Is not Pompeius the tool of coarse schemers? Do they not pray for proscriptions and confiscations and abolition of debt? Will there be any peace, any happiness in life, so long as we call ourselves freemen yet endure the chains of a despotism worse than that of the Parthians?"

Cæsar shook his head. "You do not know what you say. Every man has his own life to live, his own death to die. Quintus Drusus, I have dared many things in my life. I defied Sulla; it was boyish impetuosity. I took the unpopular and perilous side when Catilina's confederates were sent to their deaths; it was the ardor of a young politician. I defied the rage of the senate while I was a prætor; still more hot madness. I faced death a thousand times in Gaul, against the Nervii, in the campaign with Vercingetorix; all this was the mere courage of the common soldier. But it is not of death I am afraid, be it death on the field of battle or death at the hands of an executioner, should I fall into the power of my enemies. I fear myself."

Cæsar was no longer resting on the bank. He was pacing to and fro with rapid, nervous steps, crushing the dry twigs under his shoes, pressing his hands together behind his back, knitting and unknitting his fingers.

Drusus knew enough to be aware that he was present as a spectator of that most terrible of all conflicts — a strong man's wrestle with his own misgivings. To say something that would ease the shock of the contest — that was the young man's compelling desire, but he felt as helpless as though he, single-handed, confronted ten legions.

"Oh! Imperator," he cried, "do not desert us. Do not desert the commonwealth! Do not hand us back to new ruin, new tyrants, new wars! Surely the gods have not led you thus far and no farther! But yesterday you said they were leading us. To-day they still must guide! To you it has been given to pull down and to build up. Fail not! If there be gods, trust in them!"

Cæsar shook himself. His voice was harsh.

"I must accomplish my own fate!" he said; and then, in a totally different tone: "Quintus Drusus, I have been a coward for the first time in my life. Are you ashamed of your general?"

"I never admired you more, Imperator."

"Thank you. And will you go aside a little, please? I shall need a few moments for meditation."

Drusus clambered part way up the slope and seated himself under a stunted oak tree. The light was growing stronger. The east was overshot with ripples of crimson and orange, blending into lines each more gorgeous than a moment before. The wind was chasing in from the bosom of the Mediterranean and driving the fleeting mists up the little valley. The hills were springing out of the gloom; the thrushes were swinging in the boughs overhead and pouring out their morning song. Out from the camp the bugles were calling the soldiers for the march; the baggage trains were rumbling over the bridge. But still below on the marge lingered the solitary figure, now walking, now motionless, now silent, now speaking in indistinct monologue. Drusus overheard only an occasional word, " Pompeius, poor tool of knaves! I pity him! I must show mercy to Cato if I can! Sulla is not to be imitated! The republic is fallen; what I put in its place must not fall." Then, after a long pause, " So this was to be my end in life — to destroy the commonwealth; what is destined, is destined! " And a moment later Drusus saw the general coming up the embankment.

"We shall find horses, I think, a little way over the bridge," said Cæsar; "the sun is nearly risen. It is nine miles to Ariminum; there we can find refreshment."

The imperator's brow was clear, his step elastic, the fatigues of the night seemed to have only added to his vigorous good humor. Antiochus met them, evidently relieved of a load of anxiety. The three approached the bridge; as they did so a little knot of officers of the rear cohort rode up and saluted. The golden rim of the sun was just glittering above the eastern lowlands. Cæsar put foot upon the bridge. Drusus saw the blood recede from his face, his muscles contract, his frame quiver. The general turned to his officers.

ROME

"Gentlemen," he said quietly, "we may still retreat, but if we once pass this little bridge, nothing is left for us but to fight it out in arms."

The group was silent, each waiting for the other to speak. At this instant a mountebank piper sitting by the roadway struck up his ditty, and a few

THE APPIAN WAY IN CÆSAR'S TIME

idle soldiers and wayfaring shepherds ran up to him to catch the music. The man flung down his pipe, snatched a trumpet from a bugler, and, springing up, blew a shrill blast. It was the Advance. Cæsar turned again to his officers. "Gentlemen," he said, "let us go where the omens of the gods and the iniquity of our enemies call us! *The die is now cast!*"

And he strode over the bridge, looking neither to the right hand nor to the left. As his feet touched the dust of the road beyond, the full sun touched the horizon, the landscape was bathed with living, quivering gold, and the brightness shed itself over the steadfast countenance, not of Cæsar the proconsul, but of Cæsar the insurgent.

The Rubicon was crossed.

Abridged from "A Friend to Cæsar"[1]

Rubicon (roō'bĭ kŏn). — **Gaul**: a Roman province, a part of which comprises what is to-day France. — **Pompey** (pŏm'pĭ). — **legion** (lē'jụn): a division of the Roman army; a legion contained from three thousand to six thousand men. — **Ravenna** (rạ vĕn'a). — **prætorium** (prē tō'rĭ ụm): the general's tent. — **tribunes** (trĭb'ūnz) **of the plebs** (plēbz): tribunes of the people; officers elected to protect the people. — **Sulla** (sŭl'ạ): a cruel self-appointed dictator of Rome, a little older than Cæsar. — **Curio** (kū'rĭ ō). — **Pompeius** (pŏm pē'yụs). — **Magnus** (măg'nụs): the Great, a title given to Pompey by Sulla. — **Drusus** (droō'sus). — **centuries**: divisions of the Roman army, generally containing a hundred men each. — **Imperator** (ĭm pē rā'tọr): commander, leader. — **Ariminum** (a rĭm'ĭ nŭm). — **cohort** (kō'hôrt): one of the ten divisions of a legion. — **Antiochus** (ăn tī'ō kụs). — **miasmal** (mī ăz'mạl): malarial. — **pænula** (pē'nụ lạ): cloak. — **Cisalpine** (sĭs ăl'pīn): on this side of the Alps; used with reference to Rome, meaning "on the south side of the Alps." — **Marcus Antonius** (mär'kụs ăn tō'nĭ ụs): Mark Antony. — **proscription**: the publication of names of persons condemned to death. — **prætor** (prē'tọr): a magistrate next below the consul in rank. — **Catilina** (kăt ĭ lī'nạ): a Roman conspirator. — **Nervii** (nĕr'vĭ ī): a tribe of the Belgians in Gaul. Cæsar's conquest of them was the most remarkable victory of his Gallic (găl'ĭk) campaigns. — **Vercingetorix** (vẽr'sĭn jĕt'ō rĭks): the chief of the Nervii. — **Cato** (kā'tō): a Roman patriot. — **The Advance**: a military bugle call.

[1] Copyright, 1900, by The Macmillan Company.

ANTONY'S ADDRESS TO THE ROMANS ON THE DEATH OF CÆSAR

WILLIAM SHAKESPEARE

Mark Antony obtains permission from Brutus to speak at Cæsar's funeral. His intention is to stir up the Romans to mutiny, but he begins in a very careful way by speaking kindly of Brutus and the others. Brutus had made a speech just before Antony's, explaining why they had thought it necessary to assassinate Cæsar.

ANTONY

Friends, Romans, countrymen, lend me your ears;
I come to bury Cæsar, not to praise him.
The evil that men do lives after them;
The good is oft interrèd with their bones;
So let it be with Cæsar. The noble Brutus
Hath told you Cæsar was ambitious:
If it were so, it was a grievous fault,
And grievously hath Cæsar answered it.
Here, under leave of Brutus and the rest, —
For Brutus is an honorable man;
So are they all, all honorable men, —
Come I to speak in Cæsar's funeral.
He was my friend, faithful and just to me:
But Brutus says he was ambitious;
And Brutus is an honorable man.
He hath brought many captives home to Rome,
Whose ransoms did the general coffers fill:

Did this in Cæsar seem ambitious?
When that the poor have cried, Cæsar hath wept:
Ambition should be made of sterner stuff:
Yet Brutus says he was ambitious;
And Brutus is an honorable man.
You all did see that on the Lupercal
I thrice presented him a kingly crown,
Which he did thrice refuse: was this ambition?
Yet Brutus says he was ambitious;
And, sure, he is an honorable man.
I speak not to disprove what Brutus spoke,
But here I am to speak what I do know.
You all did love him once, not without cause:
What cause withholds you, then, to mourn for him?
O judgment! thou art fled to brutish beasts,
And men have lost their reason. Bear with me;
My heart is in the coffin there with Cæsar,
And I must pause till it come back to me.

First Citizen
Methinks there is much reason in his sayings.

Second Citizen
If thou consider rightly of the matter,
Cæsar has had great wrong.

Third Citizen
                  Has he, masters?
I fear there will a worse come in his place. . . .

ROME

Fourth Citizen
Now mark him, he begins again to speak.
Antony
But yesterday the word of Cæsar might
Have stood against the world; now lies he there,
And none so poor to do him reverence.
O masters, if I were disposed to stir
Your hearts and minds to mutiny and rage,
I should do Brutus wrong, and Cassius wrong,
Who, you all know, are honorable men:
I will not do them wrong; I rather choose
To wrong the dead, to wrong myself and you,
Than I will wrong such honorable men.
But here's a parchment with the seal of Cæsar;
I found it in his closet, 't is his will:
Let but the commons hear this testament, —
Which, pardon me, I do not mean to read, —
And they would go and kiss dead Cæsar's wounds
And dip their napkins in his sacred blood,
Yea, beg a hair of him for memory,
And, dying, mention it within their wills,
Bequeathing it as a rich legacy
Unto their issue.
Fourth Citizen
We'll hear the will: read it, Mark Antony.
All
The will, the will! we will hear Cæsar's will. . . .

ANTONY
You will compel me, then, to read the will?
Then make a ring about the corpse of Cæsar,
And let me show you him that made the will.
Shall I descend? and will you give me leave?

SEVERAL CITIZENS
Come down.

SECOND CITIZEN
Descend.

THIRD CITIZEN
You shall have leave. (*Antony comes down.*)

FOURTH CITIZEN
A ring; stand round.

FIRST CITIZEN
Stand from the hearse, stand from the body.

SECOND CITIZEN
Room for Antony, most noble Antony.

ANTONY
Nay, press not so upon me; stand far off.

SEVERAL CITIZENS
Stand back; room; bear back.

ANTONY
If you have tears, prepare to shed them now.
You all do know this mantle: I remember
The first time ever Cæsar put it on;
'T was on a summer's evening, in his tent,

ROME

That <u>day</u> he overcame the Nervii:
Look, in this place ran Cassius' dagger through:
See what a rent the envious Casca made:
Through this the well-belovèd Brutus stabbed;

JULIUS CÆSAR

And as he plucked his cursèd steel away,
Mark how the blood of Cæsar followed it,
As rushing out of doors, to be resolved
If Brutus so unkindly knocked, or no;

For Brutus, as you know, was Cæsar's angel:
Judge, O you gods, how dearly Cæsar loved him!
This was the most unkindest cut of all;
For when the noble Cæsar saw him stab,
Ingratitude, more strong than traitors' arms,
Quite vanquished him: then burst his mighty heart;
And, in his mantle muffling up his face,
Even at the base of Pompey's statua,
Which all the while ran blood, great Cæsar fell.
O, what a fall was there, my countrymen!
Then I, and you, and all of us fell down,
Whilst bloody treason flourished over us.
O, now you weep; and, I perceive, you feel
The dint of pity: these are gracious drops.
Kind souls, what, weep you when you but behold
Our Cæsar's vesture wounded? Look you here,
Here is himself, marred, as you see, with traitors.

First Citizen
O piteous spectacle!

Second Citizen
O noble Cæsar!

Third Citizen
O woful day!

Fourth Citizen
O traitors, villains!

ROME

First Citizen
O most bloody sight!

Second Citizen
We will be revenged.

All
Revenge! About! Seek! Burn! Fire! Kill! Slay!
Let not a traitor live!

Antony
Stay, countrymen.

First Citizen
Peace there! hear the noble Antony.

Second Citizen
We 'll hear him, we 'll follow him, we 'll die with him.

Antony
Good friends, sweet friends, let me not stir you up
To such a sudden flood of mutiny.
They that have done this deed are honorable:
What private griefs they have, alas, I know not,
That made them do it: they are wise and honorable,
And will, no doubt, with reasons answer you.
I come not, friends, to steal away your hearts:
I am no orator, as Brutus is;
But, as you know me all, a plain blunt man,
That love my friend; and that they know full well
That gave me public leave to speak of him:
For I have neither wit, nor words, nor worth,

Action, nor utterance, nor the power of speech,
To stir men's blood: I only speak right on;
I tell you that which you yourselves do know;
Show you sweet Cæsar's wounds, poor poor dumb
    mouths,
And bid them speak for me: but were I Brutus,
And Brutus Antony, there were an Antony
Would ruffle up your spirits and put a tongue
In every wound of Cæsar that should move
The stones of Rome to rise and mutiny.

ALL

We'll mutiny.

FIRST CITIZEN

We'll burn the house of Brutus.

THIRD CITIZEN

Away, then! come, seek the conspirators.

ANTONY

Yet hear me, countrymen; yet hear me speak.

ALL

Peace, ho! Hear Antony. Most noble Antony!

ANTONY

Why, friends, you go to do you know not what:
Wherein hath Cæsar thus deserved your loves?
Alas, you know not: I must tell you, then:
You have forgot the will I told you of.

ROME

ALL
Most true. The will! Let's stay and hear the will.

ANTONY
Here is the will, and under Cæsar's seal.
To every Roman citizen he gives,
To every several man, seventy-five drachmas.

SECOND CITIZEN
Most noble Cæsar! We'll revenge his death.

THIRD CITIZEN
O royal Cæsar!

ANTONY
Hear me with patience.

ALL
Peace, ho!

ANTONY
Moreover, he hath left you all his walks,
His private arbors and new-planted orchards,
On this side Tiber; he hath left them you,
And to your heirs forever, common pleasures,
To walk abroad and recreate yourselves.
Here was a Cæsar! when comes such another?

FIRST CITIZEN
Never, never. Come, away, away!
We'll burn his body in the holy place,
And with the brands fire the traitors' houses.
Take up the body.

SECOND CITIZEN

Go fetch fire.

THIRD CITIZEN

Pluck down benches.

FOURTH CITIZEN

Pluck down forms, windows, anything.

[*Exeunt Citizens with the body*

ANTONY

Now let it work. Mischief, thou art afoot,
Take thou what course thou wilt!

Abridged from "Julius Cæsar"

answered: atoned for. — **general coffers**: public treasury. — **the Lupercal** (lū'pēr kăl): feast of Lupercus (lū pēr'kŭs). — **the commons**: the common people. — **testament**: will. — **napkins**: handkerchiefs. — **issue**: children. — **hearse**: bier. — **Cassius**; **Casca** (kăs'ka): two of the conspirators. — **Brutus**: one of the chief conspirators and Cæsar's dear friend. — **as rushing**: as if rushing. — **resolved**: convinced. — **most unkindest**: the double superlative, though not considered good English to-day, was common in Shakespeare's time. — **statua** (stăt'ū a): statue. — **dint**: pressure, power. — **I am no orator**: Antony knows he is a consummate orator. — **every several man**: every individual man. — **seventy-five drachmas**: about $11. — **On this side Tiber**: a mistake of Shakespeare's. Cæsar's gardens were on the other side of the Tiber from Rome. — **walk abroad**: walk abroad in. — **forms**: benches. — **Exeunt** (ĕk'sĕ ŭnt): Latin for "They go out."

THE ROMAN FORUM

Isabel Lovell

The Forum was the "place out of doors" (and that is what the word *forum* means) of which the Romans were most proud. It was an open, oblong space through which passed several narrow streets, and round which were many of the principal buildings of the city. It was used for many purposes: as a marketplace, where all kinds of things were bought and sold, from a sack of meal to a necklace of finest gold; as a court of law, where men were tried and judged, from the pickpocket to the traitor of his country; as a meeting place, where friends came together, both the common citizens and the men of high degree; and as a place of entertainment, where the people amused themselves with games and where feasts were given in honor of great events, such as the birthday of an emperor or the triumph of a victorious general.

The Forum contained a greater number of beautiful buildings and monuments than any other place of its size and kind in all the world, for although it was not much wider or longer than one of our city blocks, there were on the Forum the senate house, the prison, the tabularium, or record building, and the rostra, or platform from which orators spoke; also several temples and basilicas, or law courts, and statues and triumphal arches and columns raised in honor of famous men or of great national events. The Forum was the center of the city of Rome, as the city was the center of the nation.

RUINS OF THE ROMAN FORUM

In the days of Augustus Cæsar a magnificent monument was placed in the center of the Forum; it was a column of bronze covered with gold, set on a base of beautifully carved marble, and it was called the Golden Milestone. On it, by order of Augustus, were marked the names and the distances of the chief towns on all the highways that led from the thirty-seven gates of Rome. So the

ROME

Golden Milestone told of the greatness of the Romans, the most famous of all the road builders of the world, who by these wonderful highways bound each town to Rome itself and made the center of the nation mighty.

Abridged from "Stories in Stone from the Roman Forum"

tabularium (tăb ū lā′rĭ ŭm). — **rostra** (rŏs′trạ): Latin for "the beaks," so called from the beaks of captured war vessels with which the platform was adorned. — **basilicas** (bạ sĭl′ĭ kạz): oblong buildings having a broad main portion flanked with colonnaded aisles, or porticoes, used for the sittings of tribunals, or courts.

THE GOLDEN MILE-STONE

Henry Wadsworth Longfellow

Leafless are the trees; their purple branches
Spread themselves abroad, like reefs of coral,
      Rising silent
In the Red Sea of the winter sunset.

From the hundred chimneys of the village,
Like the Afreet in the Arabian story,
      Smoky columns
Tower aloft into the air of amber. . . .

On the hearth the lighted logs are glowing,
And like Ariel in the cloven pine-tree
      For its freedom
Groans and sighs the air imprisoned in them. . . .

Each man's chimney is his Golden Mile-Stone;
Is the central point, from which he measures
      Every distance
Through the gateways of the world around him.

In his farthest wanderings still he sees it;
Hears the talking flame, the answering night-wind,
      As he heard them
When he sat with those who were, but are not.

ROME

Happy he whom neither wealth nor fashion,
Nor the march of the encroaching city,
    Drives an exile
From the hearth of his ancestral homestead.

RUINS OF THE HOUSE OF THE VESTALS, ROMAN FORUM

We may build more splendid habitations,
Fill our rooms with paintings and with sculptures,
    But we cannot
Buy with gold the old associations!

Afreet (ăf'rēt): an evil demon, or monster, in Arabian stories. — **Ariel** (ā'rĭ ĕl): see Shakespeare's "Tempest."

THE COLOSSEUM

Charles Dickens

When we came out of the church, we said to the coachman, "Go to the Colosseum." In a quarter of an hour or so he stopped at the gate, and we went in.

It is no fiction, but plain, sober, honest truth, to say (so suggestive and distinct is it at this hour) that for a moment — actually in passing in — they who will may have the whole great pile before them as it used to be, with thousands of eager faces staring down into the arena, and such a whirl of strife and dust going on there as no language can describe.

Its solitude, its awful beauty, and its utter desolation strike upon the stranger the next moment like a softened sorrow, and never in his life, perhaps, will he be so moved and overcome by any sight not immediately connected with his own affections and afflictions.

To see it crumbling there, an inch a year, its walls and arches overgrown with green, its corridors open to the day, the long grass growing in its porches, young trees of yesterday springing up on its ragged parapets and bearing fruit (chance produce of the seeds dropped there by the birds who build their nests within its chinks and crannies); to see its pit of fight filled up with earth, and the peaceful cross planted in the center; to climb into its upper halls and look down on ruin, ruin, ruin all about it, — the triumphal arches of Constantine, Septimius Severus,

THE ARCH OF CONSTANTINE

and Titus, the Roman Forum, the palace of the Cæsars, the temples of the old religion, fallen down and gone, — is to see the ghost of old Rome, wicked, wonderful old city, haunting the very ground on which its people trod.

It is the most impressive, the most stately, the most solemn, grand, majestic, mournful sight conceivable. Never, in its bloodiest crime, can the sight of the gigantic Colosseum, full and running over with the lustiest life, have moved one heart as it must move all who look upon it now — a ruin. God be thanked — a ruin!

Abridged from " Pictures from Italy "

Colosseum (kŏl′o̢ sē′u̢m). — **Constantine** (kŏn′stan tĭn). — **arena** (a̢ rē′na̢): the central part of Roman amphitheaters, in which the combats of gladiators or of wild beasts occurred. — **arches of Constantine, Septimius Severus, Titus** (tī′tu̢s): great triumphal arches erected by the Roman emperors of these names, to celebrate their victories.

THE COLOSSEUM

ANDROCLUS AND THE LION

A Roman Tradition

There was once a slave named Androclus, who was so ill treated by his master that at length he said to himself: " It is better to die than to live in such hardship. I am determined to run away. If I am taken again, I know that I shall be punished with a cruel death, but it is better to die at once than to live in misery. If I escape, I must betake myself to deserts and woods inhabited only by beasts, but they cannot use me more cruelly than I have been used by my fellow creatures."

Having formed this resolution, he left his master's house and hid himself in a thick forest, which was some miles distant from the city. But here the unhappy man found that he had only escaped from one kind of misery to experience another. He wandered about all day through a vast and trackless wood, where his flesh was continually torn by thorns and brambles. He grew hungry but could find no food in this dreary solitude. At length he was ready to die with fatigue, and lay down in despair in a large cavern which he found by accident.

He had not long lain quiet in the cave before he heard a dreadful noise, which seemed to be the roar of some wild beast. He started up with the intention of escaping, and had already reached the mouth of the cave, when he saw coming toward him a lion of immense size, who prevented any possibility of retreat. Androclus now believed his death to be inevitable, but to his great astonishment the beast advanced toward him at a gentle pace, without any sign of enmity or rage, and uttered a kind of mournful wail, as if he wanted the assistance of the man.

From this circumstance Androclus, who was naturally of a resolute disposition, acquired courage to examine his strange guest. He saw, as the lion approached him, that he seemed to limp upon one of his legs, and that the foot was extremely swelled, as if it had been wounded. Acquiring still more fortitude from the gentle demeanor of the beast, he went up to him and took hold of the wounded paw as a surgeon would examine a patient. He then perceived that a thorn of uncommon size had penetrated the ball of the foot and was the cause of the swelling and lameness which he had observed. Androclus found that the beast, far from resenting this familiarity, received it with the greatest gentleness and seemed to invite him to proceed. He therefore extracted the thorn and, pressing the swelling, discharged a quantity of pus, which had been the cause of the lion's pain.

ROME

As soon as the beast felt himself thus relieved, he began to testify his joy and gratitude by every expression within his power; he jumped about like a spaniel, wagged his enormous tail, and licked the feet and hands of his physician. Nor was he contented with these demonstrations of kindness; from this moment Androclus became his guest, and the lion never went forth in quest of food without bringing home the results of the chase and sharing them with his friend. In this savage state of hospitality the man continued to live for several months. At length, wandering through the woods, he met a company of soldiers sent out to apprehend him, and was by them taken prisoner and conducted back to his master. The Roman laws of that time being very severe against slaves, he was tried and found guilty of having fled from bondage, and, as a punishment for his so-called crime, he was sentenced to be torn in pieces by a furious lion, which had been kept many days without food in order to inspire him with additional rage.

When the fatal day arrived, the unhappy man was exposed, unarmed, in the midst of a spacious arena inclosed on every side, round which many thousands of people were assembled to view the spectacle. Presently a fearful roar was heard, which struck the spectators with horror, and a monstrous lion rushed out of a den, the door of which was set open, and darted forward with erected mane and flaming eyes, and jaws that gaped like an open sepulchre. A breathless silence instantly prevailed. All eyes were turned directly upon the victim, whose destruction now appeared inevitable, but the pity of the multitude was soon converted into astonishment when they beheld the lion, instead of destroying his defenseless prey, crouch submissively at his feet, fawn upon him as a faithful dog would fawn upon his master, and rejoice over him as a mother that unexpectedly recovers her child. The governor of the town, who was present, called out with a loud voice and ordered Androclus to explain to them this mystery.

Androclus then related to the assembly every circumstance of his adventures in the forest, and concluded by saying that the very lion which now stood before them had been his friend and entertainer in the woods. All the people present were delighted with the story and with the knowledge that even the fiercest beasts are capable of being softened by gratitude and moved by love, and they all asked the governor of the place for the pardon of the unhappy man. This was immediately granted to him, and he was also presented with the lion that had twice saved his life.

THE BAY OF NAPLES AND VESUVIUS

THE BAY OF NAPLES

The Bay of Naples is one of the most beautiful and one of the most interesting spots on earth. Graceful hills rise from its waters on all sides, and towering four thousand feet above it, stretches the volcano Vesuvius, a smoking torch by day, a pillar of fire by night. Just below Vesuvius lie two buried cities, Pompeii and Herculaneum, now only just emerging from the deep deposit of lava streams and devastating ashes that covered them utterly more than eighteen hundred years ago.

Palaces and villas, vineyards and gardens, adorn the sloping hillsides. On one of these slopes was the home of the poet Vergil. But Mt. Vesuvius is always the background of every picture of the Bay of Naples; it is the presiding genius of the place.

THE BLUE GROTTO, CAPRI

In the Bay of Naples lies the island of Capri, once the home of the Cæsars. The emperor Augustus was especially fond of it and made of it a dream of delight. He left the island to his successor Tiberius, and Tiberius built upon the cliffs of Capri twelve splendid palaces, each vying with the others

ROME

in magnificence, and all of them lavishly adorned with statues, theaters, groves, and gardens. In each of these palaces he lived a month in turn throughout the year, thus making the island for the time the center of the civilized world.

One of the most attractive features of Capri is its wonderful Blue Grotto. The opening to the cave is so small that the visitor has to lower his head when the boat enters, and only a very small boat can enter the grotto. But within, walls, roof, and water are of the most beautiful shade of blue, such as no painter in the world can reproduce. The oar of the boat seems in the water like a blade of sapphire; the hand dipped in the waves gleams like silver; the opening to the cave, through which alone the light can enter, appears like the sun rising from a sea of turquoises.

The visitor does not linger long, however, in the Blue Grotto, for if the sea should become violent, he might have to remain in the cave till the wind changed and the waves went down. Travelers have sometimes been detained thus for twenty-four hours.

Pompeii (pŏm pā′yē). — **Herculaneum** (hẽr kû lā′nĕ ųm). — **Capri** (kä′prē). — **Tiberius** (Tī bē′rĭ ųs).

DRIFTING

Thomas Buchanan Read

    My soul to-day
    Is far away,
Sailing the blue Vesuvian bay;
    My wingèd boat,
    A bird afloat,
Swings round the purple peaks remote; —

    Round purple peaks
    It sails, and seeks
Blue inlets and their crystal creeks,
    Where high rocks throw,
    Through deeps below,
A duplicated golden glow.

    Far, vague, and dim,
    The mountains swim;
While on Vesuvius' misty brim,
    With outstretched hands,
    The gray smoke stands
O'erlooking the volcanic lands.

    There Ischia smiles
    O'er liquid miles;
And yonder, bluest of the isles,

ROME

    Calm Capri waits,
      Her sapphire gates
Beguiling to her bright estates.

    No more, no more
    The worldly shore
Upbraids me with its loud uproar:
     With dreamful eyes
     My spirit lies
Under the walls of Paradise.

Ischia (ēs′kyä): an island near the entrance to the Bay of Naples.

CAPRI

THE HOUSE OF GLAUCUS

BULWER-LYTTON

There is much to draw the traveler to the neighborhood of Naples — much besides the cloudless sky, the violet valleys, and the orange groves of the south of Italy. The beautiful Bay of Naples still spreads its blue waters, and the fatal mountain of Vesuvius still breathes forth smoke and fire, as they did eighteen hundred years ago, when Pompeii was in its glory.

And to-day, a few miles outside Naples, the traveler can walk the deserted streets of beautiful Pompeii and view the ruins of the houses, the temples, and the theaters of a city that eighteen hundred years ago was full of life. It is not hard to repeople in imagination those streets and houses.

Pompeii was a tiny city. It was like a toy, a plaything, compared with the great city of Rome, then at the height of its magnificence. But Pompeii contained in miniature all that made Rome the wonder of the world. The streets were filled with gay little shops, all opening directly upon the sidewalks. Sparkling fountains at every vista threw their spray upwards in the summer air. Gay groups of people in purple robes collected about the attractive shops. Slaves passed to and fro with buckets of bronze upon their

A POMPEIAN COURTYARD

heads. Country girls stood on street corners with baskets of fruit and brilliant flowers. Pompeii had its tiny palaces, its baths, its forum, its theater, and its circus, while crowded in the Bay of Naples were many merchant ships and pleasure boats.

In this city lived a young man named Glaucus, who seemed to have every blessing in the world but one. He had beauty and health, genius and wealth, but he was not free. He was a slave because he had been born in Athens, at that time subject to Rome. But Glaucus had an ample inheritance, and he loved to travel. His house in Rome was the wonder of all lovers of art. His best-loved home, however, was at Pompeii, its walls covered with paintings, its floors of mosaics, a fairylike mansion with every elaborate finish of grace and ornament.

The ancient houses of Pompeii were built like the Roman houses. You entered by a small vestibule into a hall. Around three sides of this hall were doors that led into bedrooms. At the end of the hall on either side were two rooms for the women, and in the center a square, shallow reservoir for rain water. Near this reservoir were placed the images of the household gods. Beyond the hall was a dining room, separated from the hall only by a row of columns. Beyond this were rooms for the slaves, opening on a small garden in the center, and beyond this garden was the kitchen. At Pompeii the houses were usually only one story high. The rooms were small, for the people lived largely in the hall or the garden. The main portions of the house opened into each other, separated only by columns, and from the front vestibule you had a view of the hall, richly paved and painted, the banquet room, and the garden beyond.

The house of Glaucus was one of the smallest but one of the most beautiful in Pompeii. On the floor of the vestibule was the picture of a dog in mosaic, and under it the words *Cave canem*, or " Beware the dog." In his hall the walls were rich with paintings, as were also those in the banquet room. In the little garden bloomed the rarest of flowers. The dining table was of highly polished wood inlaid with silver. Around it were three couches, for the Romans half sat, half reclined at their meals, leaning upon the left elbow. The couches were of bronze inlaid with gold, and on them were laid thick quilts covered with elaborate embroideries. All who saw it admitted that there was not a more beautiful house in all Pompeii.

Adapted from " The Last Days of Pompeii "

Glaucus (glau´kŭs). — **Cave canem** (kā´vĕ kā´nĕm).

GAINING WINGS

Edna Dean Proctor

A twig where clung two soft cocoons
    I broke from a wayside spray,
And carried home to a quiet desk
    Where, long forgot, it lay.

One morn I chanced to lift the lid,
    And lo! as light as air,
A moth flew up on downy wings
    And settled above my chair!

A dainty, beautiful thing it was,
    Orange and silvery gray,
And I marveled how from the leafy bough
    Such fairy stole away.

Had the other flown? I turned to see,
    And found it striving still
To free itself from the swathing floss
    And rove the air at will.

" Poor little prisoned waif," I said,
    " You shall not struggle more ";
And tenderly I cut the threads,
    And watched to see it soar.

ROME

Alas! a feeble chrysalis
    It dropped from its silken bed;
My help had been the direst harm —
    The pretty moth was dead!

I should have left it there to gain
    The strength that struggle brings:
'T is stress and strain, with moth or man,
    That free the folded wings!

THE BLIND FLOWER GIRL

Bulwer-Lytton

Just where the porticoes of a light and graceful temple threw their shade stood a young girl. She had a flower basket on her right arm and in her left hand a small three-stringed lyre, to whose low tones she was singing a wild and half-barbaric air. At every pause in the music she lifted her flower basket, inviting the people to buy. Many a coin was dropped into the basket, either in compliment to the music or in pity of the singer, for she was blind.

"It is my poor Thessalian," said Glaucus to a friend who was walking with him; "I have not seen her since my return to Pompeii. Hush! her voice is sweet; let us listen."

>Buy my flowers — O buy — I pray!
> The blind girl comes from afar;
>If the earth be as fair as I hear them say,
> These flowers her children are!
>Do they her beauty keep?
> They are fresh from her lap, I know;
>For I caught them fast asleep
> In her arms an hour ago,
>With the air which is her breath —
>Her soft and delicate breath —
> Over them murmuring low!

NYDIA
After the painting by Bodenhausen

On their lips her sweet kiss lingers yet,
And their cheeks with her tender tears are wet.
For she weeps — that gentle mother weeps —
(As morn and night her watch she keeps,
With a yearning heart and a passionate care)
To see the young things grow so fair;
   She weeps — for love she weeps;
   And the dews are the tears she weeps,
   From the well of a mother's love!

"I must have a bunch of violets, Nydia," said Glaucus, pressing through the crowd and dropping a handful of small coins in her basket.

The blind girl started forward. "So you are returned," she said in a soft voice; "Glaucus is returned."

"Yes, child, I have been in Pompeii but a few days. My garden wants your care; you will visit it, I trust, to-morrow. No hands but those of Nydia shall wind any garlands for my house."

The blind girl smiled, but did not answer.

"So she is a client of yours," said Glaucus's friend, as they went away.

"Yes. Does she not sing prettily? She interests me, the poor slave! Besides, she is from the land of Olympus; she is of Thessaly."

Adapted from "The Last Days of Pompeii"

Thessalian (thĕ sā'lĭ an): one born in Thessaly (thĕs'a lĭ), a section of Greece. — **Nydia** (nĭd'ĭ a). — **client** (klī'ent): a person in ancient Rome who was under the protection of another of superior rank and influence. — **Bodenhausen** (bō'den hou'zen).

A ROMAN MOTHER AND DAUGHTER
After the painting by J. Coomans

THE BOY AND THE ANGEL

Robert Browning

Morning, evening, noon and night,
"Praise God!" sang Theocrite.

Then to his poor trade he turned,
Whereby the daily meal was earned.

Hard he labored, long and well:
O'er his work the boy's curls fell.

But ever, at each period,
He stopped and sang, "Praise God!"

Then back again his curls he threw,
And cheerful turned to work anew.

Said Blaise, the listening monk, "Well done;
I doubt not thou art heard, my son:

"As well as if thy voice to-day
Were praising God, the Pope's great way.

"This Easter Day, the Pope at Rome
Praises God from Peter's dome."

Said Theocrite, "Would God that I
Might praise him that great way, and die!"

Night passed, day shone;
And Theocrite was gone.

ROME

With God a day endures alway,
A thousand years are but a day.

God said in heaven, "Nor day nor night
Now brings the voice of my delight."

Then Gabriel, like a rainbow's birth,
Spread his wings and sank to earth;

Entered, in flesh, the empty cell,
Lived there, and played the craftsman well;

And morning, evening, noon and night,
Praised God in place of Theocrite.

And from a boy, to youth he grew;
The man put off the stripling's hue;

The man matured and fell away
Into the season of decay:

And ever o'er the trade he bent,
And ever lived on earth content.

(He did God's will; to him, all one
If on the earth or in the sun.)

God said, "A praise is in mine ear;
There is no doubt in it, no fear:

" So sing old worlds, and so
New worlds that from my footstool go.

"Clearer loves sound other ways:
I miss my little human praise."

Then forth sprang Gabriel's wings, off fell
The flesh disguise, remained the cell.

'T was Easter Day: he flew to Rome,
And paused above Saint Peter's dome.

In the tiring-room close by
The great outer gallery,

With his holy vestments dight,
Stood the new Pope, Theocrite:

And all his past career
Came back upon him clear,

Since when, a boy, he plied his trade,
Till on his life the sickness weighed;

And in his cell, when death drew near,
An angel in a dream brought cheer:

And rising from the sickness drear,
He grew a priest, and now stood here.

To the East with praise he turned,
And on his sight the angel burned.

"I bore thee from thy craftsman's cell,
And set thee here; I did not well.

ANGEL WITH VIOLA
After the painting by Melozzo da Forlì

" Vainly I left my angel-sphere,
Vain was thy dream of many a year.

" Thy voice's praise seemed weak; it dropped —
Creation's chorus stopped!

" Go back and praise again
The early way, while I remain.

" With that weak voice of our disdain,
Take up creation's pausing strain.

" Back to the cell and poor employ:
Resume the craftsman and the boy!"

Theocrite grew old at home;
A new Pope dwelt in Peter's dome.

One vanished as the other died:
They sought God side by side.

Theocrite (thē´ō krīt). — **Blaise** (blāz). — **Gabriel** (gā´brī ĕl): one of the archangels. — **season of decay**: old age. — **remained the cell**: the empty cell was left; the angel was gone. — **tiring-room**: attiring room, dressing room. — **dight** (dīt): dressed, adorned. — **praise again the early way**: become a boy again working at your trade. — **while I remain**: while I remain here as the Pope. — **a new Pope**: the angel Gabriel. — **one vanished**: the angel went back to God. — **Viola** (vĭ ō´la). — **Melozzo da Forli** (mä lŏt´sŏ dä fŏr lē´): an Italian painter born in Forli.

THE ERUPTION OF VESUVIUS

Bulwer-Lytton

Glaucus, through the evil powers of an enemy, had been accused of a dreadful crime. Since he was not a free-born Roman citizen (such could not be put to death by barbarous methods), he was cast into prison to await his fate, which was, to be thrown to the lions in the amphitheater. Ione, his betrothed, and Nydia, the poor slave girl, were in despair of saving his life.

"Glaucus the Athenian, thy time has come," said a loud and clear voice; "the lion awaits thee."

The lion had been kept without food for twenty-four hours, and during the whole morning had shown a singular uneasiness. Its bearing seemed more that of fear than of rage. It hung its head, snuffed the air through the bars, then lay down again.

Glaucus stood in the arena, waiting. The door of the lion's cage was opened, but to the astonishment of all the beast paid no attention to the prisoner. It circled round and round the place, seeking some way to escape. At length it crept with a moan back into its cage.

Suddenly a loud cry was heard at one of the entrances. The eyes of the crowd seemed drawn upward and beheld with dismay a vast vapor shooting from the summit of Vesuvius in the form of a gigantic pine tree, the trunk blackness, the branches fire!

There was a dead, heart-sunken silence, through which there broke the roar of the lion. Then there rose shrieks of women; the men stared at each other but were dumb. At that moment they felt the earth shake beneath their feet; the walls of the theater trembled. An instant more and the mountain cloud seemed to roll toward them, dark and rapid, like a torrent, casting from its bosom a shower of ashes mixed with fragments of burning stone.

The crowd turned to fly, each dashing, pressing, crushing against the other. Glaucus had been led by the officers of the arena into a small cell, when an impatient cry was heard without. The throng gave way, and the blind girl flung herself at his feet, sobbing, "I have found thee; I am not too late." The officers fled with the rest, and Glaucus and Nydia swiftly paced the perilous streets. They hastened to the home of Ione. The darkness increased so rapidly that it was with difficulty they could guide their steps. The flower-wreathed columns seemed to reel and tremble. Breathless, Glaucus rushed forward, shouting aloud the name of Ione, and at length heard her voice in wondering reply. To seize Ione in his arms — to hurry from the mansion — seemed to him the work of an instant! The three hastened onward. Alas! whither? They saw not a step before them; the blackness became utter. The mighty mountain now cast up

POMPEII AND VESUVIUS

columns of boiling water. At frequent intervals the streams, blended and kneaded with the half-burning ashes, fell like seething mud upon the streets.

The cloud which had scattered so deep a murkiness over the day had now settled into a solid and

ERUPTION OF VESUVIUS IN 1872

impenetrable mass, but in proportion as the blackness gathered did the lightnings around Vesuvius increase in their vivid and scorching glare. Nor was their horrible beauty confined to the usual hues of fire; no rainbow ever rivaled their varying and prodigal dyes, now brightly blue as the most azure depth of a southern sky, now of a livid and snakelike green, darting restlessly to and fro as the folds of an enormous serpent, now of a lurid and intolerable crimson, gushing forth through the columns of smoke, far and wide, and lighting up the whole city from arch to arch, then suddenly dying into a sickly paleness, like the ghost of their own life.

In the pauses of the showers you heard the rumbling of the earth beneath, the groaning waves of the tortured sea, or the hissing murmur of the escaping gases through the chasms of the distant mountain.

The ashes in many places were already knee-deep, and the boiling showers which came from the steaming breath of the volcano forced their way into the houses, bearing with them a strong and suffocating vapor. In some places immense fragments of rock, hurled upon the house roofs, bore down along the streets masses of confused ruin which yet more and more obstructed the way.

Here and there in more public places, such as the porticoes of temples and the entrances to the forum, citizens had endeavored to place rows of torches, but these rarely continued long — the showers and the winds extinguished them.

Frequently, by the momentary light of these torches, parties of fugitives encountered each other, some hurrying toward the sea, others flying from the sea back to the land. Wild, haggard, ghastly with supernatural fears, these groups gazed at each other, but without the leisure to speak, to consult, to advise.

Through this awful scene did Glaucus make his way, accompanied by Ione and the blind girl. Suddenly a rush of hundreds, in their path to the sea, swept by them. Nydia was torn from the side of Glaucus, who with Ione was borne rapidly onward, and when the crowd (whose forms they saw not, so thick was the gloom) were gone, Nydia was still separated from their side. Glaucus shouted her name. No answer came. They retraced their steps — in vain; they could not discover her; it was evident that she had been swept along by the human current. Their friend, their preserver, was lost! for hitherto Nydia had been their guide. Her blindness rendered the scene familiar to her alone. Accustomed through a perpetual night to tread the windings of the city, she had led them unerringly toward the seashore, by which they had resolved to hazard an escape. Now, which way could they wend? All was rayless to them — a maze without a clue.

Advancing, as men grope for escape in a dungeon, they continued their uncertain way. At the moments when the volcanic lightnings lingered over the streets, they were enabled by that awful light to steer and guide their progress; yet little did the view it presented to them cheer or encourage their path. Cinder and rock lay matted in heaps, and ever as the winds swept howling along the street, they bore sharp streams of burning dust and sickening and poisonous vapors.

Meanwhile Nydia, when separated by the throng from Glaucus and Ione, had in vain endeavored to regain them. In vain she raised that plaintive cry so peculiar to the blind. Again and again she returned to the spot where they had been divided, to be dashed aside in the impatience of distraction. Who in that hour spared one thought to his neighbor? At length it occurred to Nydia that as it had been resolved to seek the seashore for escape, her most probable chance of rejoining her companions would be to persevere in that direction. Guiding her steps, then, by the staff which she always carried, she continued, with incredible dexterity, to avoid the masses of ruin that encumbered the path, and to take the nearest direction to the seaside.

The sea had retired far from the shore, and they who had fled to it had been so terrified by this and by the sound of the huge stones cast from the mountain into the deep that they had returned again to the land.

And now new fugitives arrived; from them Nydia learned that Glaucus was still in the forum. Silently she glided through the throng. She gained the forum

— the arch; she stooped down; she felt around; she called on the name of Glaucus.

A weak voice answered, "Who calls on me?"

"Arise; follow me! Take my hand! Glaucus, thou shalt be saved!"

In wonder and sudden hope Glaucus arose; "Nydia? Ah! thou, then, art safe!" The tender joy of his voice pierced the heart of the blind girl.

Half carrying Ione, Glaucus followed his guide. After incredible perseverance they gained the sea and joined a group who, bolder than the rest, resolved to hazard any peril rather than continue in such a scene. In darkness they put forth, but as they cleared the land the channels of molten fire on the mountain threw a redness over the waves.

Meanwhile the showers of dust and ashes fell into the wave and scattered their snows over the deck. Far and wide, borne by the winds, those showers descended upon the remotest climes, startling even the swarthy African, and whirled along the antique soil of Syria and of Egypt.

Abridged from "The Last Days of Pompeii"

Ione (ī ō'nē). — **lurid** (lū'rĭd): appearing like fire seen through smoke.

HOW PLINY SAVED HIS MOTHER

During all this time my mother and I remained at Misenum, my uncle having left us. For many days a trembling of the earth had been noticed. This did not alarm us much, as it is quite an ordinary occurrence in southern Italy, but it was very violent that night and overturned everything about us.

My mother rushed into my room, where she found me rising to awaken her. We sat down in the open court of the house, which was in a small space between the buildings and the sea. I was but eighteen years of age at the time, and I do not know whether I was courageous or foolish, but I took up a book — my Livy — and amused myself with turning over its pages.

Just then a Spanish friend of my uncle's joined us and reproved me for my careless security.

Though it was now morning, the light was faint. Buildings all around us were tottering, and we resolved to leave the town.

A panic-stricken crowd followed us. At a little distance from the houses we stood still in the midst of a most dreadful scene. The ground shook violently. The sea seemed to roll back upon itself and to be driven from the shores. On the other side, above Vesuvius, reared a black and dreadful cloud, broken with rapid and zigzag flashes.

Upon this my uncle's friend urged us to escape. "If your uncle were here," he said, "he would certainly wish you to survive him. Why do you delay your escape a moment?"

But we told him that as long as we were uncertain of my uncle's safety we could not think of our own. Upon this our friend left us with the greatest haste.

Soon afterwards the cloud began to descend and cover the sea. It had already hidden the island of Capri. My mother now begged me to make my escape, which, as I was young, I might easily do. She would willingly meet death herself, she said, if she might know she was not the cause of mine. But I absolutely refused to leave her and, taking her hand, compelled her to go with me. The ashes began to fall upon us, though in no great quantity. A dense mist seemed to be following us.

"Let us turn out of the highway," I said, "while we can still see; if we should fall in the road, we should be crushed to death in the dark by the crowds." We had scarcely done this when night came upon us — a blackness like that of a room when it is shut up and all the lights are put out.

You could hear the shrieks of women, the screams of children, and the shouts of men. Some were calling for their children, others for their parents or their husbands. They tried to recognize each other by the voices that replied. Some were lifting their hands to the gods, and some were convinced that there were no gods and that the end of the world had come.

It grew lighter; the light was caused not by day but by a great burst of flames from the mountain. The fire, however, fell at a distance from us.

Then again came thick blackness, and a heavy shower of ashes rained upon us. We were obliged every now and then to rise and shake them off, else we should have been buried in the heap.

At last the dreadful darkness disappeared by degrees; the real day returned. Every object on which our eyes rested was covered deep with ashes, as if with snow.

We returned to Misenum and passed an anxious night between hope and fear, for the earthquake still continued. But notwithstanding the danger we had passed, and that which still threatened us, my mother and I had no thoughts of leaving the place until we could receive some news of my uncle.

From the letter of Pliny the Younger to Tacitus

Pliny (plĭn'ĭ). — **Misenum** (mĭ sē'nŭm): a town near Pompeii. — **uncle**: Pliny the Elder, a noted scientist, who lost his life by venturing too near the mountain during this eruption. — **Livy** (lĭv'ĭ): a great Roman historian. — **Tacitus** (tăs'ĭ tŭs): a Roman historian and orator.

THE CHAMBERED NAUTILUS

Oliver Wendell Holmes

This is the ship of pearl, which, poets feign,
    Sails the unshadowed main,—
    The venturous bark that flings
On the sweet summer wind its purpled wings
In gulfs enchanted, where the siren sings,
    And coral reefs lie bare,
Where the cold sea-maids rise to sun their streaming hair.

Its webs of living gauze no more unfurl;
    Wrecked is the ship of pearl!
    And every chambered cell,
Where its dim dreaming life was wont to dwell,
As the frail tenant shaped his growing shell,
    Before thee lies revealed,—
Its irised ceiling rent, its sunless crypt unsealed!

Year after year beheld the silent toil
    That spread his lustrous coil;
    Still, as the spiral grew,
He left the past year's dwelling for the new,
Stole with soft step its shining archway through,
    Built up its idle door,
Stretched in his last-found home, and knew the old no more.

ROME

Thanks for the heavenly message brought by thee,
    Child of the wandering sea,
    Cast from her lap, forlorn!
From thy dead lips a clearer note is born
Than ever Triton blew from wreathèd horn!
    While on mine ears it rings,
Through the deep caves of thought I hear a voice
    that sings:

Build thee more stately mansions, O my soul,
    As the swift seasons roll!
    Leave thy low-vaulted past!
Let each new temple, nobler than the last,
Shut thee from heaven with a dome more vast,
    Till thou at length art free,
Leaving thine outgrown shell by life's unresting sea!

Nautilus (nau′tĭ lŭs): a shellfish, named from the Latin word for "sailor." One variety of nautilus has a spiral shell divided into several chambers by pearly partitions. — **poets feign**: the nautilus does not sail over the seas, in spite of its name. — **Siren** (sī′rĕn): a sea nymph who was supposed to lure sailors to death. — **irised** (ī′rĭst): colored like the rainbow; Iris (ī′rĭs) was the goddess of the rainbow. — **Triton** (trī′tŏn): the son of the sea god Neptune. When the ocean roared, Triton was said to be blowing his horn. — **wreathèd horn**: a spiral conch shell.

THE EXCAVATIONS AT POMPEII

In the year 79 of the Christian era the city of Pompeii was totally destroyed by an eruption of Vesuvius and buried under ashes. The site of the ancient city was discovered in 1713 by some Italian peasants who were digging for a well. Excavations have been carried on down to the present time. About half of the old city has been dug up.

Because of the layers of ashes and pumice that covered Pompeii, the ruins were kept in a remarkable state of preservation and to-day give us our most valuable information concerning ancient Roman civilization.

Just outside the city gates stood a large and beautiful villa. It was between the city and the mountain. When this place was excavated, two skeletons were found close beside the garden gate. One was evidently that of the master of the house; he had in his hand the key of the gate, and near him were about a hundred gold and silver coins. The other was evidently a slave and was stretched beside some silver vases.

Within the cellars of the house were discovered the skeletons of eighteen persons; they had lain in those ashes for seventeen hundred years. The ashes, cemented together by dampness, have taken

THE HOUSE OF PANSA, POMPEII

a perfect impression of everything on which they lay. So exact is this impression that even the texture of the cloth that once made a little girl's dress can be plainly seen. The cloth was so very fine that we know she was not a slave. The impression of jewels worn on the neck and arms is distinct, and the jewels themselves were found beside the skeletons. There were two necklaces, one set with blue stones, and four rings containing beautiful gems.

A STREET IN POMPEII

The objects found in Pompeii have been carefully preserved. Articles of furniture and objects of art that could easily be moved, such as the statuettes often found in the gardens, were ordinarily taken to the museum in Naples; a few things have been placed in the little museum at Pompeii. Now and then small sculptures have been left in a house exactly as they were found, but the necessity of keeping such houses locked, and of guarding them with especial care, has prevented the general adoption of this method of preservation.

The frescoes that adorned the walls have been wonderfully preserved, and bits of them, exquisite in form and color, have occasionally been left in the houses where they were found. The walls were made of stucco, hard and smooth as marble, and then decorated with designs of graceful lines and rich, harmonious coloring.

Upon the side of one house is rudely scratched the Greek alphabet. It must have been made by a little fellow, for the letters are only about three feet above the ground. Two other walls are marked with quotations from Vergil and from Ovid, possibly written by children on their way to school.

The remains of Pompeii shed light on countless passages of Greek and Roman writers. Literature, however, ordinarily records only that which is exceptional or striking, while here we find the surroundings of life as a whole, the humblest details being presented to the eye. From the study of Pompeii, as from no other source outside the pages of classical writers, we come to understand the life of the ancient Roman.

pumice (pŭm′ĭs): a very light volcanic stone having a loose, spongy structure. — **Ovid** (ŏv′ĭd): a Latin writer. — **Pansa** (păn′zạ).

SELECTIONS FROM MARCUS AURELIUS

Marcus Aurelius Antoninus, born in Rome in the year 121, was loved and admired even in his own day as no other Roman emperor ever was. He was adopted by the emperor Antoninus, and on the death of the latter, in 161, he ascended the throne. He has been the admiration of the whole world ever since that time. He was not only great as a statesman and ruler, but his life as a private man was even more admirable. There was in him a fine simplicity, sincerity, purity, fidelity to duty, dignity, and a most potent personal charm. He shows the union of the best qualities of the man of action and the man of thought.

These few extracts from his book of "Meditations" show us his personality. This book was written during the last years of the emperor's life and under the pressure of heavy toil in the face of increasing bodily weakness and domestic sorrow. It was never intended for the public eye, but was merely his own thoughts, addressed to himself alone, because he found the writing an aid to serenity in his many afflictions. Not until the fourteenth century did it come into the possession of the world. The "Meditations" have been called "the most geniune expression in all literature of the peace of a really triumphant soul — the true peace of God."

As Antoninus, my city and country is Rome, but as a man, the universe. — *Book VI.*

Whatever is harmonious to thee is harmonious to me, O Universe. For me nothing is too early and nothing is too late which is seasonable for thee. All is fruit for me, O Nature, that thy seasons bear. From thee are all things, in thee they exist, to thee they shall return. Does the poet say, " Dear city of Cecrops," and wilt thou not exclaim, "Beloved city of God"? — *Book IV.*

"Do few things," says some one, "if you would have tranquillity." A better rule, methinks, is, "Do only what is necessary, what the reason of a social

THE TIBER AND THE CASTLE OF ST. ANGELO

being demands and in the way it directs." This brings the tranquillity that comes of doing a few things and doing them well. In each case one should ask one's self, "Is this one of the necessary things?" — *Book IV.*

Whatever any one else may do or say, I must be good; just as the emerald forever says, "Let others do or say what they please, I must remain an emerald and keep my proper luster." — *Book VII.*

Do not be ashamed to accept assistance. You should do your appointed work as a soldier storms a breach. What if you are lame and cannot scale the battlement alone? You may be able to do so with another's help. — *Book VII.*

When any one does you a wrong, set yourself at once to consider what was the point of view, good or bad, that led him astray. As soon as you see it, you will be sorry for him, not surprised or angry. It may be your own opinion of good is the same as his, or very much like it; then you will make allowance for him. Or, if you do not share his views of good and evil, you will the more easily be charitable to his mistake. — *Book VII.*

Dig within. Within you is a fountain of good, welling up perpetually if you always dig.—*Book VII.*

Whatever is beautiful owes its beauty to itself, and in itself it is complete; praise has nothing whatever to do with it, for it is made neither better nor worse by being praised.
This is true of the common forms of beauty, such as material objects, for instance, and works of art. What is truly beautiful needs nothing outside itself

ROME

MARCUS AURELIUS

to make it so, any more than law, or truth, or kindness, or self-respect. Can any of these be beautified by praise or marred by censure? Is the emerald less perfect if one praises it not? or is gold, or ivory, or purple? a lyre or a dagger? a flower or a shrub?—*Book IV.*

Watch well the grace and charm that belong even to the consequences of nature's work. For example, when a loaf of bread is baked, cracks and crevices appear in the crust, and the clefts thus produced, though not designed by the baker, are attractive and stimulate the appetite.

Figs also, when they are quite ripe, begin to crack. In ripe olives the very nearness to decay lends a peculiar beauty; so with the bending ear of corn, the frowning brow of the lion, the foam that drips from the wild boar's mouth, and many other things which, considered by themselves, are far from beautiful, yet, looked at as the consequences of nature's work, add new beauty and appeal to the soul; so that if one has sympathy with the workings of the universe, and insight into them, everything connected with them will be seen to have a beauty of its own. For eyes thus skilled to see, age also in man or woman will have its own loveliness, as well as the exquisite charms of youth.

These things will not appeal to all, but only to him who is at home with nature and her works.—*Book III.*

How goes it with your inner self? That is everything. All else, whether under your control or not, is as dust and ashes.

You have lived, man, as a citizen of the great world-city. Five years or seventy, what matters it? To every man his due, as the law allots. Why, then, protest? No tyrant gives you your dismissal, no unjust judge, but nature who led you into the city. Surely the prætor who engaged the player can dismiss him from the stage. "But," say you, "the five acts are not complete; I have played but three." Good; life's

PYRAMID OF CESTIUS IN ROME

drama, look you, is complete, then, in three. The completeness is in His hands who caused your entrance and now your dismissal; you are responsible for neither. Serenely take your leave; serene is He who gives you your discharge. — *Book XII.*

Marcus Aurelius Antoninus (au rē'lǐ ŭs ăn tō nī'nŭs). — **City of Cecrops** (sē'krŏps): Athens. Tradition makes Cecrops the first king of Athens.

MY BOOKS

Justin Huntly McCarthy

On level lines of woodwork stand
My books, obedient to my hand;
And Cæsar pale against the wall
Smiles sternly Roman over all.
Within the four walls of this room
Life finds its prison, youth its tomb:
For here the minds of other men
Prompt and deride the laboring pen;
And here the wisdom of the wise
Dances like motes before the eyes.
Outside the great world spins its way.
Here studious night dogs studious day.
A mighty store of dusty books,
Little and great, fill all the nooks,
And line the walls from roof to floor;
And I who read them o'er and o'er,
Am I much wiser than of old,
When sunlight leaped like living gold
Into my boyhood's heart, on fire
With fervid hope and wild desire;
And when behind no window bars,
But free as air I served the stars?

night dogs studious day: night hurries hard after day.

www.ingramcontent.com/pod-product-compliance
Lightning Source LLC
Chambersburg PA
CBHW031340230426
43670CB00006B/395